Winning With Strategic Marketing

Winning With Strategic Marketing

Driving Success for Startups and Small Businesses

David Altounian and Mike Cronin

BEP

BUSINESS EXPERT PRESS

Leader in applied, concise business books

Winning With Strategic Marketing: Driving Success for Startups and Small Businesses

Copyright © Business Expert Press, LLC, 2024

Cover design by Charlotte Straus

Interior design by Exeter Premedia Services Private Ltd., Chennai, India

First published in 2023 by
Business Expert Press, LLC
222 East 46th Street, New York, NY 10017
www.businessexpertpress.com

ISBN-13: 978-1-63742-549-7 (paperback)
ISBN-13: 978-1-63742-550-3 (e-book)

Business Expert Press Marketing Collection

First edition: 2023

10 9 8 7 6 5 4 3 2 1

Description

This book provides a comprehensive guide to marketing for leaders of startups, small-, and mid-sized businesses, empowering them to expand and evolve their enterprises.

It offers a framework to create a fundamental marketing plan that helps business leaders understand and thrive in a competitive environment. The framework offers a step-by-step process to build a plan that will enable readers to acquire new customers, maintain existing clientele, anticipate competitors' moves, showcase product uniqueness, grasp pricing strategies, refine branding messages, and select appropriate metrics to evaluate progress.

By adhering to our straightforward approach, readers will learn how to develop a marketing strategy that will help generate sales, profit, and customer satisfaction.

Keywords

marketing; strategic marketing; value creation; value capture; profit; upstream marketing; downstream marketing; market segmentation; marketing funnel; competitive analysis; customer acquisition; customer retention; customer loyalty; customer advocacy; channels; metrics; pricing strategies; branding strategies; target audience; product positioning; market research; digital marketing; content marketing; social media marketing; search engine marketing; email marketing; product pricing; product planning; promotion; advertising; entrepreneurial marketing; startups

Contents

Preface

The idea for this book emanated from two different circumstances happening around the same time: a consulting project for a local ice cream sandwich shop and classroom and academic department discussions at a university in Austin, Texas. These experiences led to the concern that strategic marketing methods were being taught in advanced marketing classes but were less accessible to those without marketing degrees or to people whose main interest is the business they run or the services they provide.

Much of the marketing how-to information available to that audience today is around digital marketing, social media, and getting "more eyeballs" for a product or service. There also seems to be a growing gap in the understanding of what marketing is and the role that it plays in the success or failure of a business. These marketing education materials are important, and we don't wish to diminish their value, but they only represent a portion of the marketing approach. To build successful, profitable, and sustainable businesses, understanding and executing effective marketing strategies are required.

The challenge that we decided to undertake was to introduce some of the fundamental marketing strategy approaches by combining elements from commonly taught academic models and theories into a worksheet tool and to explain how to build the elements of a marketing strategy with the tool through chapters designed for people without experience in marketing. Our goal is to introduce the basic principles and fundamentals of marketing strategy and, hopefully, provide a starting point for additional interest and deeper exploration of marketing.

While the authors of this book—a former marketing executive and current academic and a journalist—have endeavored to write this in a way that is easily accessible for the nonmarketing person, no book like this can be successful without illustrations to visualize the concepts. Our thanks go to our graphic artist, Charlotte Straus, for her work in doing this well.

This is neither intended to be a heavy academic tome on marketing concepts nor do we claim that this represents all that is needed to build a successful marketing program. It's intended to be a structured way to begin understanding how to use strategic marketing to improve and enhance your business.

David Altounian and Mike Cronin

CHAPTER 1

What Is Marketing?

All businesses do marketing, even when not well-planned or thoughtfully executed. From Fortune 500 companies with multilevel teams numbering in the hundreds to mom-and-pop operations with a student intern assigned to posting on social media, marketing plays a critical role.

Marketing Is Everywhere, and It Isn't New

The discipline of marketing has been around for centuries, well before modern technology became the norm.

SAVE ONE THIRD
By Buying of the Makers
We are actual manufacturers—not a commission house. We can and do save our customers one third on retail prices by selling direct to user and cutting out all dealers' profits. All our goods carry our guarantee. Our free illustrated catalogue shows a greater assortment of carriages and harness than any dealer can show you. Send for it.
THE COLUMBUS
CARRIAGE AND HARNESS COMPANY,
COLUMBUS, OHIO.

$48.75 Buys an $85.00 Union Runabout
with ⅞-in. Rubber Tires, best hickory wheels, high arch, long distance axle, oil tempered springs, piano finish body. This is a beautiful job of first quality, fully guaranteed, and worth nearly double our special factory price. We ship it to you for examination without a cent in advance if desired, and allow
30 DAYS' FREE TRIAL
If not satisfactory we agree to refund your money. You save dealers' profits. We make 156 other styles from $26.50 to $150. Harness $5 to $60. Write to-day for our 100-page Illustrated free catalogue and special offer.
UNION BUGGY COMPANY, 516 Saginaw St., PONTIAC, MICH.

Figure 1.1 Two examples of early advertising from 1904

Here are two examples of marketing from the turn of the century in print advertisements. But the ads themselves are merely one component of marketing. Take a closer look. You will notice that in the first ad, the Columbus Carriage and Harness Company talks about its product features. The company also describes a distribution advantage: customers can get a one-third discount by ordering directly from the manufacturer.

In the second ad, the Union Buggy Company also contains pricing, as well as a promotion: Customers may try out the product for 30 days free of charge.

All those ad characteristics are parts of marketing. Someone at each company decided which features of those products would appeal to consumers. Someone decided how the products would be priced and sold. And someone decided how to promote the products to encourage buyers to pick them over the competitors' offerings. Those decisions encompass only some of marketing's essential elements.

Today, 120 years after those ads, with social media and e-commerce now commonplace across many sectors to accelerate the promotional aspects of marketing, the basic principles of strategic marketing remain. Even as the manner in which companies conduct business continues to evolve, marketing's fundamental frameworks and theoretical models, such as the Four Ps of Marketing or Porter's Five Forces, still are relevant.

An examination of what occurred in California's grocery industry during the mid-1970s illustrates this. Larger, independent supermarkets and regional grocery chains such as Safeway and Vons began competing with small, local grocery stores. That fierce competition resulted in many smaller stores folding.

As competition for customers increased, those running the grocery stores needed to:

- Understand who their customers were—and the unique needs of those customers. As chains expanded, the needs of the customers in specific neighborhoods became important to attract or keep customers. Doing that, the grocers were practicing the marketing tenets of segmentation and preference.
- Stock the products those customers wanted, in other words, the grocers' product offerings.
- Be competitive with other grocery stores in product selection, pricing, and the quality of products offered. That process is what marketers call differentiation and is determined through a process called "competitive analysis."

- Set the pricing of their products in a way that attracted customers and generated a store profit. This is what's commonly known as "pricing strategy."
- Create enough awareness and interest to lure customers into the store.
- Distribute weekly advertising to area potential customers, which is the marketing practice of "placement."
- Create a store layout that maximized the possibility of a customer making a purchase, which represented the marketing activities of driving customer "awareness" and "consideration."

To design that store layout, grocers employed several tactics. They strategically displayed sales items at the front of the aisles. They placed produce and dairy products in a way that could simplify the customers' search and selection process and encourage the purchase of additional items. They created brilliant displays in refrigerated cases, ensuring that items such as cheeses, meats, and produce looked fresh and inviting.

Fifty years later, grocery store operators still engage in these activities. Digital tools and technology have vastly improved the execution, but the underlying processes remain the same. Stories of massive corporations swallowing local, independent businesses can be found in every industry. But examples still exist of small or specialty grocery stores succeeding against much larger competition. This shows the effectiveness of strategic marketing, even when the scales appear to be imbalanced.

Grocery stores are among the most successful types of businesses in adopting new and emerging technologies. They are constantly innovating to improve their customer service and marketing strategies with methods such as loyalty programs and real-time price changes using digital shelf tags.

The COVID-19 pandemic accelerated changes in the way that customers buy groceries with the growth of curbside pickup and online ordering and delivery. In 2009, H-E-B, one of the largest grocery chains in Texas, created a plan for operating in a pandemic based on the H1N1 flu virus that afflicted Asia. The chain began implementing elements of the plan in early 2020 at the beginning of the pandemic. The rollout of curbside pickup allowed H-E-B to broaden its appeal to customers.

The grocery sector also is an example of how even mature industries continually evolve to meet customer preferences and expectations. Whole Foods Market is an example of a grocery store chain that identified customer segments interested in products that are organic and from fair-trade companies and support health and wellness trends. Whole Foods built a multibillion-dollar business by serving those segments.

Since we all shop at grocery stores and likely will continue to do so for years to come, what they do in the marketing realm is instructive. We'll return to grocery stores throughout this book to demonstrate how small- and mid-sized businesses capably employ strategic marketing in a variety of scenarios.

Understanding how to harness the power of good marketing can help small- and mid-sized businesses compete in the marketplace, improve profitability, and increase customer satisfaction. Marketing is a major contributor to the success or failure of a business. Great businesses do great marketing.

A lot of confusion surrounds what marketing is. Even people who work in the field have disagreements about what constitutes marketing and what doesn't. Under the general umbrella of "marketing," a variety of functions exist. The list includes strategic marketing, brand marketing, product marketing, channel marketing, marketing communications, advertising, and public relations.

Banking is comparable to marketing in that many components compose the broader term: retail banking, commercial banking, investment banking, and electronic banking to name a few.

In order to make sense of the word "marketing," it is important to understand the term's various definitions throughout the years.

Marketing is:

- Both a science and an art. One of the leading academics in the field, Philip Kotler, Northwestern University Kellogg School of Management professor emeritus of marketing, said, "Marketing is the science and art of exploring, creating, and delivering value to satisfy the needs of a target market at a profit."

- A function and set of processes. The American Marketing Association (AMA) in 2004 defined marketing as "an organizational function and a set of processes for creating, communicating, and delivering value to customers and for managing customer relationships in ways that benefit the organization and its stakeholders."
- A set of offerings that have value. The AMA updated its definition in 2017: "Marketing is the activity, set of institutions, and processes for creating, communicating, delivering, and exchanging offerings that have value for customers, clients, partners, and society at large."

While these are helpful, we offer the following:

Marketing is the use of a set of activities, tools, and processes to create value (getting the desired product at the expected price) for your customers while capturing value (profit) for your organization. In simpler terms, marketing is creating value for your customers while capturing value for your company.

This means that all activities a business conducts should aim to create more value for its customers than the competition is creating while maximizing the value for the organization, whether it be profit or other benefits (e.g., nonprofits and B Corporations may look for donations or volunteer hours).

Let's look back at the grocery store example. One of the major mechanisms of adding value for customers while also capturing value for the business is the weekly flier found at the entrance to most stores.

The weekly flier serves several purposes:

- It makes customers aware of items they might not have considered prior to seeing the flier.
- It encourages the purchase of more products by offering promotional pricing. This increases the total sale amount, capturing more profit from the higher sales revenue.
- It creates opportunities for additional item purchases. For example, a sale on seafood could lead to the purchase of spices, side dishes, and other items that the customer might not have planned to buy when entering the store.

Marketing Is Not Sales, but It Can Be a Sales Accelerator

A common, accepted definition of "sales" is "the exchange of a commodity for money; the action of selling something." The term relates to the process of managing the actual transaction between a firm and the customer. Although marketing is commonly confused with sales, the two disciplines are distinct.

Take our grocery store example. The butcher behind the counter is involved in selling meat. The butcher engages in a friendly exchange with the customer, explains the different meat cuts available for purchase, and provides suggestions on how to prepare the cuts of meat. Then the butcher measures, wraps, and delivers the final product to the customer.

The butcher does not decide which meat products to carry in the store, how they should be priced based on cost and competitive analysis, or how they should be displayed. Those are marketing decisions. The butcher assists the customer at the point of sale.

Marketing concentrates on the factors that provide the best opportunity for the butcher behind the counter *and* the customer to have a profitable transaction.

Doing Good Marketing Can Help Your Business Succeed

To be successful, business leaders should, at a minimum:

- Generate sales
- Cultivate happy, loyal customers
- Earn profit

Optimizing all three creates a healthy, growing business. Reaching just two of those goals, however, may be easy for organizations to attain but could actually destroy long-term value.

Selling a terrible product at a competitive price could have short-term benefits—make sales and generate profit, for example—but it will not create happy customers. Selling good products at a low price will create happy customers, but it probably will not generate profit.

While it may seem a little academic and theoretical, it's important to look at marketing as a discipline all on its own. It's not sales, and it's not advertising. Although advertising is one component of marketing, marketing is a unique segment of business management that is, at its core, focused on creating and capturing value. Externally, it does this by concentrating on things like customers and competition. Internally, it does this by focusing on things like product-feature requirements, pricing, and messaging.

To illustrate, consider how Ram Charan, a globally known advisor to CEOs and companies for decades and an award-winning teacher at Northwestern University, described marketing in his 2004 book, *Profitable Growth Is Everyone's Business.*

Charan defined "upstream marketing" as the company's long-term strategy and plans around the industry and market; customer needs and wants; and the company's products, competition, and vision for how to lead in a market. He identified "downstream marketing" as the shorter-term external marketing activities needed to drive sales. These include advertising, social media, public relations, search-engine activities, pricing, promotions, and marketing communications. Strategic marketing is typically focused on upstream marketing activities. Downstream marketing is often planned and managed by those in an organization's channel marketing, digital marketing, advertising, marketing communications, and public relations departments.

Many small businesses outsource downstream marketing to marketing firms and consultants that turn strategic marketing planning into advertising and marketing communications materials and advertising campaigns. If you've ever watched the TV show *Mad Men*, you may recall that the strategic marketing team members were those brand executives listening to the pitches from the creative team. The show's fictional firm, Sterling Cooper Draper Pryce, executed downstream marketing.

Understanding strategic marketing helps provide business leaders with the basic tools and processes to build a balanced, successful, and

Internal team members
Supply chain partners
Prospective customers
Potential partners

UPSTREAM

- Identifying who the customer is
- Defining customer wants/needs
- Competitive analysis
- Product/service definition
- Pricing planning
- Value proposition
- Distribution planning

DOWNSTREAM

- Advertising
- Promotion strategies
- Product messaging
- Publicity/public relations
- Events
- Sales materials and supports
- Content marketing

Target customers
Current customers
Distribution partners
Your sales team

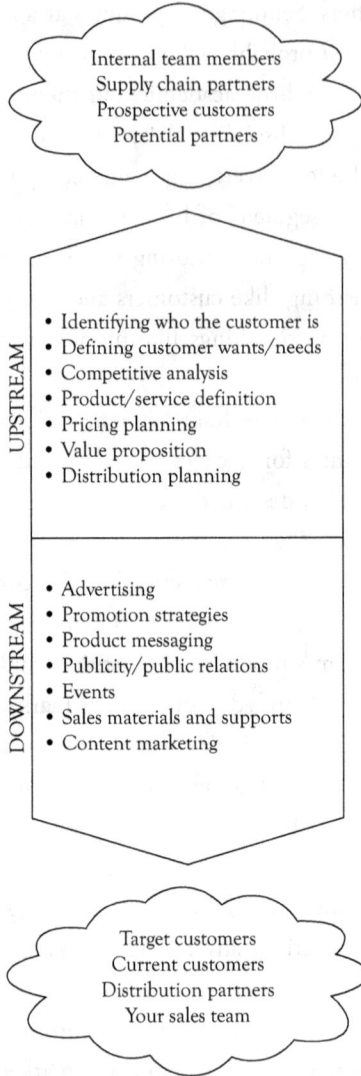

Figure 1.2 Upstream and downstream activities

growing business. A marketing strategy should accomplish one or more of the following objectives:

- Increase brand awareness by encouraging prospective customers to select you because of your reputation or capability.
- Generate sales by driving demand for your product or services.

- Establish thought leadership by developing a market position as the expert resource for products or services.
- Increase customer engagement by developing ongoing, profitable relationships with your customers.

In the chapters that follow, we will look at the elements that enhance market position and success by focusing on strategic marketing (upstream marketing). We'll also briefly touch on messaging and advertising (downstream marketing). This approach will help you understand how to better understand your market environment, target the right customers for your product or services, and establish the right pricing, messaging, and approaches to better serve your customers and your bottom line.

But first, we need to introduce you to the model that drives the economics for great marketing.

Key takeaways from this chapter:

1. The origins of marketing predate the digital era, with the inception of modern marketing beginning in the 1800s.
2. The goal of marketing is to create value for your customers while capturing value for your company.
3. Marketing is an umbrella term that encompasses various functions, such as strategic marketing, product marketing, channel marketing, advertising, and marketing communications.
4. While marketing and sales are distinct concepts and activities, effective marketing contributes to sales outcomes.
5. Upstream marketing pertains to a company's long-term plans and strategies related to customer segmentation, product planning, pricing, and message development. Downstream marketing refers to short-term external marketing activities aimed at driving sales.

CHAPTER 2

Understanding Business Economics—The Value Equation

Now that you know marketing is more than just advertising and messaging, let's look at how it contributes to the overall success of a business.

One of the most significant things to understand about strategic marketing is the importance of balancing the needs and wants of the customer with the needs and wants of the business. A company can create incredible products with lots of bells and whistles, but if the customer doesn't find value in additional features, then the company is adding costs to products that customers don't want or expect to pay for.

By the same token, it is important to be aware of the trap of reducing the price simply to satisfy the customer. Doing so could result in customers paying less than it costs the company to make and sell the product.

Consider utensils and sauces included by restaurants for takeout and delivery services. It's not unusual to find many small condiment containers and utensil packages at the bottom of your meal order. Many customers find those items annoying and throw them away. Smart restaurants are now asking the customer—through an ordering app during the initial order or at pickup—whether they want those items.

This is good business and good marketing. After all, these items are not free for the restaurant. They are costs that could impact the overall profit for the restaurant. These costs could easily add up to many dollars a night. That's hundreds of dollars a month out of the profits and into the trash. Including unwanted condiments and utensils in every bag adds no value to the customer. Worse, it represents lost value (profit) to the restaurant. Asking the customer about their preferences ensures the restaurant delivers what the customer wants while increasing the profit from that sale.

This isn't to say that it's unnecessary to include condiments and utensils. It depends on the customer segment and on what the customer needs and expects. We're presenting this example simply to highlight how a restaurant can optimize costs and customer satisfaction with small tweaks to the ordering process.

Successful marketing aims to support the delivery of the right product at the right price for the customer while optimizing the costs to make and deliver the product. This need for balance is explained using the marketing value equation.

While "adding value" and "capturing value" may seem like abstract terms, they are keys to building a successful, growing business. Businesses add value when they provide a benefit to a customer that meets or exceeds the customer's expectations. Companies frequently refer to this as "delighting the customer." For example, Jason's Deli, a popular, casual-dining restaurant headquartered in Beaumont, Texas, provides free self-serve, soft-serve ice cream to customers who dine in. This little extra bonus goes a long way in delighting customers, adds very little cost to the transaction, and may allow Jason's Deli to charge a slight premium for its offerings relative to comparable casual-dining restaurants. The free ice cream could attract more families, youth teams, and other groups—all as a result of following the marketing mantra of "delighting the customer."

If you are providing good value to your customers, then they likely will be happy and loyal to your business. If you are capturing value appropriately, then you should be generating a profit and growing the company. Understanding what is behind each of these terms is key to using the tools and frameworks that we will cover later in this book. First, though, it's important that you grasp the concept of the marketing value equation, which helps define the elements of marketing that drive the creation and capture aspects more clearly.

In economic terms, the marketing role is all about managing the business to create surpluses in both customer satisfaction and company profit. By creating value for the customer, the business can positively influence customer satisfaction. If the perceived benefit to the customer is greater than the price they would expect to pay, then the surplus results in higher customer satisfaction.

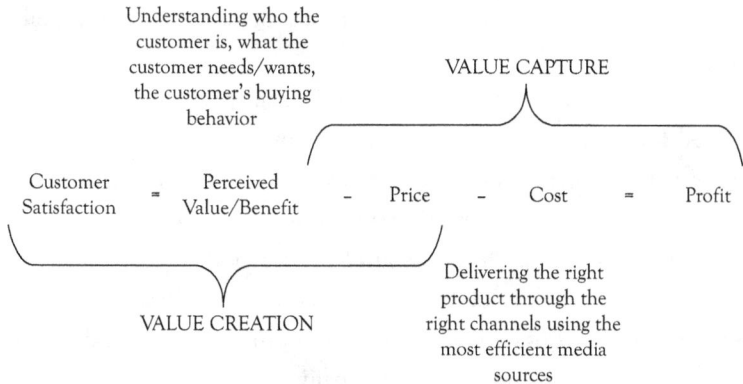

Figure 2.1 The marketing value equation

There are always two sides to this equation. One is the value-creation side, which is where the product or service that you offer creates value for your customer. The other is the value-capture side, which is where the business generates profit by capturing value from the transaction.

Let's say you go to a restaurant for the first time and see a steak dinner on the menu for $50. If you order the steak dinner at that price, then you likely expect the benefit to be a large, well-prepared steak with some side dishes and bread. If you order the steak, and the steak meets the expectation of being well proportioned, tender, well flavored, and appropriately cooked, the restaurant has likely met expectations. In that case, the perceived benefit is equal to the price.

If the steak is smaller than expected, is overcooked, or is somehow less fulfilling than expected, then the restaurant has not created value for you. Your satisfaction as a customer will be reduced. The price is greater than the received perceived benefit.

However, if your steak is done correctly, the sides are well sized, and the service by the waitstaff is highly attentive, then the restaurant could potentially exceed your expectations, which results in higher customer satisfaction. In other words, the perceived benefit is greater than the charged price.

The goal of marketing is to create value for customers. But it's easy to do this and still lose money. If the restaurant sells the dinner for $50, but the cost of the product and the service for the dinner is $50, then the restaurant is not generating a profit. It is not capturing value. The goal always is to balance creating value for the customer with capturing value for the business.

So how do we capture value? Value is frequently calculated as the price charged for a product or service minus the overall costs to produce and deliver that product or service. If the costs are lower than the price paid by the customer, then the resulting surplus is called profit.

Marketing's goal is to create surpluses for both the customer and the company. These can be measured as customer satisfaction (positive perceived benefit considering the price) and profit (the price paid by the customer minus the costs to the company to produce and supply the product).

Value Creation

Let's break down each of the components of the equation, starting with value creation. The most important aspect to understand about creating value for customers is the area of the customers' perceived benefit. To understand the benefits expected by the customer, it's imperative that the strategic marketer know who the paying customer is. Not everyone is a customer or prospective customer. In the same vein, not everyone who uses a product or service is the actual customer.

Marketers who sell sugary breakfast cereals often make those products to appeal to children. The children aren't the actual customers; however, the parents are. The marketer has to consider the perceived benefits of the product user, in this case, the children, as well as the actual buyer of the product, in this case, the parents. Not all parents are buyers of sugary cereal. Some will only buy "healthy" breakfast cereals like muesli or oatmeal. Some prefer low-cost cereal. Some have no preference. Identifying and characterizing the different types of customers, and sometimes users, is called segmentation.

Segmenting customers allows the marketing team to understand the specific needs and wants of each group of customers. It also allows for things such as analyzing price sensitivity, determining where those customers shop to buy products, what media they use to get information about the products, which social media sites they use, and other information specific to that group of customers. Based on this information, those responsible for marketing can put together a hypothesis about what customers expect from a product or service, the anticipated price points, the competition that is trying to attract those customers, and how best to reach those customers through advertising or social media.

Price

The marketer's goal is to set the price that returns the most profit for the company while maintaining customer satisfaction. Put another way, the marketer must set the price at a level that the majority of purchasers consider to be fair. It's a fool's errand to try to set a price that seems appropriate to everyone. Not everybody has the same perception of what they consider "expensive." There will always be some customers who consider the price for a product inexpensive and some who consider it expensive. Your goal is to find the expected price range that will be acceptable to the majority of the target customers.

To establish the appropriate price, it's important to have a clear understanding of who the customer is. Knowing the customer segment allows for price testing with potential customers in that segment.

Four things must be considered when setting price:

- The costs to produce and sell the product or service
- The desired profit from selling the product or service
- The willingness or capability of the targeted customer segment to pay that price
- The competitors' prices compared to yours

Consider setting the price for a fruit smoothie. If the cost of the ingredients to make the smoothie—known as the cost of goods sold in financial terms—is two dollars, and the goal is to make a dollar of profit on every smoothie sold, which would be a 50 percent gross margin, then the selling price target would be three dollars. This is normally where many businesspeople stop the pricing work, but it's incomplete. This would be only the target price.

The next step is to evaluate whether customers in your segment would be willing to pay three dollars. This is done through basic primary research. The smoothie marketer could take samples of the smoothie to prospective customers in that segment, ask how much they would pay, and analyze the results. More sophisticated pricing research incorporates focus groups, statistical evaluation of results, and test pricing, but for a small- or mid-sized business, this isn't practical or necessary.

A simple way to do this is by sampling prospective customers, tracking their responses, and analyzing the results as averages or on a bell curve to set the price. The key thing for the marketer to ensure is that the sampling is completed with prospective customers. If the target market segment is high school and college students, then that is who should be sampled. If the target segment is suburban consumers, then that is who should be sampled. These two groups have different spending capabilities and purchasing patterns.

After setting the price target and identifying the price range that would appeal to target customers, the final step is to compare the target price with the competitors selling a similar product and adjust the price as necessary.

If the competition sells the smoothie at three dollars, but your product has better ingredients, such as organic fruit, then maybe a premium of $0.30 would be appropriate. If so, then $3.30 would be a 10 percent premium compared to the competition. However, if your competition has a known brand and your product is new, then perhaps a 10 percent discount on your price would be appropriate. The setting of price requires constant review and balance among three areas of consideration, as we'll now outline.

Perceived Benefits and Expectations

Another important reason for understanding customer segmentation is that different customers have different expectations for products and services. Take our smoothie product example. A target customer segment of high school and college students most likely would care about the size of the smoothie and the flavor. They may be less interested in the actual ingredients, which would explain the popularity of the faux chocolate shakes at many fast-food restaurants. A more mature demographic, such as suburban parents, may care more about the source of the ingredients and the quality of the product. Segmentation is one place where categorizing based on demographic attributes (such as age, sex, race, and education level) and psychographic attributes (such as personal interests, values, and opinions) is critical.

Offering a product targeted at the fast-food segment with high-priced organic smoothies likely would not meet the expectations of that fast-food consumer. Conversely, offering a mass-produced smoothie at a lower cost likely would not be well received by the health-oriented parent customer segment. It's important to understand these benefits or expectations because they have a tremendous impact on customer satisfaction.

Measuring Customer Satisfaction: The Net Promoter Score

If the goal is creating value for your customers, then it is important to be able to measure it. After all, a customer whose expectations are met or exceeded will likely have a high level of satisfaction. Measuring customer satisfaction is an excellent way to understand how you are delivering on the promise of your product or service. It can also provide insight into necessary modifications or changes to your marketing plan, your product or service offering, or your pricing.

It is unlikely and actually may be indicative of giving up some profit opportunity to have off-the-charts positive customer satisfaction all the time. In fact, if you are consistently delighting the customer, then it could be that your pricing is too low and that you may be giving up value (profit) for the business. Customer satisfaction is not driven by price alone; it's driven by the price in relation to the perceived expectation. A company with low-priced products can have a much lower satisfaction rate than a company with similar products priced at higher levels if the perceived benefit is more effectively delivered by the higher-priced offerings.

One common way to measure this satisfaction level is the Net Promoter Score (NPS), which asks customers to rate companies or products on a simple scale: How likely are you to recommend the brand to a friend or colleague? The scale ranges from 0 to 10. In general, customers who provide a rating of six or less are considered detractors (unsatisfied), customers who rate a seven or eight are neutral (satisfied), and customers who rate 9 or 10 are very satisfied and are considered promoters (delighted).

How to Calculate a Net Promoter Score

The overall NPS is generated by subtracting the percentage of detractors from the percentage of promoters. The overall score range is –100 to 100. That is, if 100 percent of your respondents rank your firm as six or less, then you have an NPS score of –100. If you have 30 percent of your surveyed customers as detractors, 25 percent are neutral, and 45 percent are promoters, then you have an NPS score of 15. This is calculated as 45 percent promoters subtracted from the 30 percent detractors equals an NPS score of 15. The 25 neutral votes have no effect on the score. In general, any NPS score that is above 0 is considered positive, a score above 50 is considered very good, and above 70 is considered exceptional. Below zero is an indication that you are not delivering adequate value for your customers and likely have a marketing problem!

Measuring customer satisfaction isn't about just getting a high score. It's more about understanding how your customers perceive your product offering, the messaging about what the product promises, and the price set relative to the customer's expectations. Good strategic marketers are always evaluating customer satisfaction because it indicates the value that the customer is receiving from your company and the likelihood that they will return and recommend the brand.

While the NPS score approach is valuable for measuring the general customer satisfaction levels with your company, it's also a great way to think about customer perception at the individual customer level. After all, if a customer visits the steak restaurant, and they rate the meal at a four, then it should be pretty obvious that they likely aren't going to give a positive review online or recommend the restaurant to friends. On the other hand, if they are willing to give a 9 or a 10 score, then this is someone who is likely to share the experience and promote the restaurant to others. A goal for marketing should be to delight customers and get high scores.

Even without the formality of measuring using a process such as NPS, it's imperative that those responsible for the marketing efforts pay attention to the level of customer satisfaction. That can change quickly due to dynamics such as new competitors, competitive price actions, or quality issues.

Value Capture

The firm also has a goal of being profitable and generating positive cash flow (money generated after supporting operations and capital expenditures). That's the profit that actually goes back to the owners or investors of the company. The more profit that can be generated in a transaction—price minus cost—the more money that is available to the business. The more efficient a company can be in reaching and supporting customers, the lower the costs of acquiring and supporting the sale. Consequently, more money will go back to the company and increase profit.

The goal is to offer the service or product that customers expect, let them know about it, and get them to purchase it—all with the least amount of marketing cost. Then the business must provide after-purchase support in a cost-effective way, minimizing expenses and maximizing profit.

Price

In setting prices, it's important to understand the customer's expectations. There are several ways to set pricing. It's important to include all components of the product or service that the customer will be charged for. This is what the customer will use in evaluating the fairness of the price set by the company.

For example, say you purchase a car for $30,000 but then have to pay $10,000 for a three-year warranty. You will value that car differently than you would have had you purchased it for $40,000 with a three-year warranty included. If the marketer doesn't explicitly communicate that the $40,000 vehicle includes the warranty, then your perception might not be what the company intended. The marketer's goal in setting a price is to get the maximum amount from the customer while still generating positive customer satisfaction.

Costs

The cost of producing and delivering the product or service is also an important component of the value-capture side of the value equation. When we talk about costs in the context of marketing, we include three major components:

- Direct product costs or the costs to produce the product
- Channel or distribution costs
- Advertising costs

Good marketing can reduce costs in all three of these areas and, more importantly, deliver more profit for the company. Poor marketing can actually *reduce* profit for the business. In this age of digital marketing and less direct customer contact, it's possible to overspend on the advertising component of the costs, which has a corrosive effect on overall profitability.

Direct product or service costs are driven by the product or service being sold. These costs include everything from features to the packaging. The fast-casual restaurant product offering for a burger would include the ingredients of the burger, the packaging, and the condiments that are offered to the customer at the point of purchase.

If a customer orders a dollar burger, then the business has to determine how to make and deliver the burger with the bun, hamburger patty, lettuce, sauce, and wrapper—and generate a profit. It may be that putting the burger in a cardboard container adds $0.10 to the cost, while a paper wrapper adds only $0.02. Providing the burger with minimum sauce may result in the burger transaction becoming unprofitable if the customer then asks for a few packages of ketchup. Each of the transaction's product components must be evaluated to understand the product costs.

Often overlooked, channel or distribution costs are the second driver of overall costs for a product or service. Retail stores, distributors, and online distribution companies like Amazon and eBay expect to make money from reselling products. The total cost from the customer perspective is the price that they pay to acquire a product, not the price that the company sets. You may have noticed this effect if you've ordered food from a restaurant through a delivery service. The added service costs, delivery fees, and the tip for the driver can push the delivery price up significantly. The final price paid is generally what the customer thinks of as the price of a meal from the restaurant. That amount factors into the perception of value received. For example, a customer may have been happy paying $11 for a burger from the menu from a delivery app, but when the delivered price ends up being almost $20 after service fees and tips, it has a direct effect on the perception of the value received by that customer. If, say, the time saved was worth the extra expense, then it's a positive perception. If not—say the customer perceives that the delivered burger was worth just $11—then it's a negative perception. It's important for the marketer to understand the distribution costs when setting the price to ensure that the final amount paid by the customer is the highest possible price without negatively affecting customer satisfaction.

The better job a marketer does in generating demand for the product and satisfying customers, the lower the distribution costs should be. If the distributor must take on the costs of advertising and driving demand for the product, then those costs will be passed on to the company. In a later chapter, we will discuss demand generation and the marketing funnel, a concept that helps businesses manage marketing communications, advertising, and the costs for the different stages of customer interest.

The distribution costs should not be a mystery. If you know where and how you are going to sell your product, then you can estimate what the distribution costs will be. These costs need to be considered as components of your overall costs before setting a price.

Advertising costs are the final set of costs in the value equation. The more efficient a marketer is in getting the prospective customer to consider purchasing the product or service, then converting that prospect to an actual customer, the lower the costs will be. The result? More profit. Many marketing books and most of the efforts around social marketing and search engine marketing are about generating awareness through low-cost, viral efforts. These efforts can increase profits by reducing the cost of acquiring a new customer.

Profit

The goal of the strategic marketer is to maximize profit. Every penny spent inefficiently is profit lost and value not captured.

When marketing blogs, agencies, and tool providers talk about metrics and key performance indicators (KPIs), they are conveying the importance of understanding the drivers of profit. Such an understanding highlights the need to track pricing, cost-driver efficiency, the effectiveness of attracting customers through advertising and communications, the ability to create value for the customer, and whether you're offering the right product or service at the right price. Doing all these things is essential to maximizing profit.

Think of strong customer satisfaction as the destination, product quality and delivery efficiency as the fuel, and the resulting positive cash as the reward. If we deliver the right product or service, reach the customer in the most efficient way, and manage product, channel, and advertising costs appropriately, the reward is higher profits and higher company value.

Understanding the drivers of value creation and value capture is key in understanding the marketing decisions to be made. Everything that happens in a business influences the value equation.

Product or service features drive both customer expectations and product costs. Distribution choices affect the final price that the customer pays, as well as the amount of money left for the company. Demand generation and advertising can improve overall profitability if the advertising works or negatively impact profitability if it costs more than was expected to reach and convert a prospect into a customer.

Paying attention to and understanding the components of the value equation are critical to building a sustainable, profitable business. While managing all of this may seem daunting, we've developed a planning framework that will help to break down the elements that contribute to the value equation in a way that will help build an actionable strategic marketing plan.

Key takeaways from this chapter:

1. The marketing value equation emphasizes the dual objectives of generating value for customers (satisfaction) and capturing value for your organization (profit).
2. It is crucial to clearly understand customers' anticipated needs and desired benefits. By delivering products and services that meet these expectations, and at a price that is equal to or lower than what they expect to pay, you can effectively create value for your customers.
3. To successfully capture value, the product or service should be offered at the maximum price that customers are willing to pay, while simultaneously optimizing the costs associated with marketing, selling, and delivering the product or service.

CHAPTER 3

Basic Marketing Frameworks and Fundamentals

Now that we've covered the value equation, it's essential to introduce you to some basic frameworks that marketers use. These are models and approaches that help conceptualize some of the less obvious, "softer" areas of marketing. Understanding them will help you build your strategic marketing plan using the framework we will share with you throughout the following chapters.

Research, analysis, and development spanning decades have improved marketing best practices. This work has led to the creation of several basic frameworks that assist marketers in planning and executing their strategies. We are hopeful that by the time you finish reading this book, you will understand the importance and value of historical marketing frameworks. You will be able to use them with digital marketing tools to reach and effectively convert customers.

With any marketing initiative, it is vital to have current, accurate information and a way to make sense of that information quickly and strategically. Frameworks help you organize and understand the information. Grasping these basic models will help you begin understanding your customers, and your business, from a marketing perspective. Most students majoring in marketing learn the structure of these frameworks early in their education. Marketing teams use them throughout the product or service lifecycles. They continuously update them as they receive new information, often provided by digital marketing tools.

Examples include Google Analytics for website traffic or Meta advertising analytics (Facebook, Instagram, etc.) for social media. Marketers may use data from these services to compare activity among different time stamps and look to see the types of content performing well.

How does this current-day marketing activity relate to frameworks?

Well, the marketing funnel explains five phases of the customer journey:

1. Awareness: How many customers are made aware of the product or service—and by what means?
2. Consideration: Once customers become aware, how many actually consider purchasing the product or service?
3. Conversion: How many prospective customers end up buying the product or service?
4. Loyalty: How do customers feel about the product or service?
5. Advocacy: Are customers satisfied enough with the offering to provide a positive review or recommend the product or service?

Google Analytics or Facebook Advertising results report three points of data that tie directly to the funnel elements:

- Impressions: How many times the ad or display has shown up on users' feeds? This supplies marketers with the total number of people who saw a product or service ad. This measure indicates awareness of the offering.
- Clicks: How many times users actually click on the display to get more information. Clicks represent the total number of users who viewed the ad—which may mean that they considered buying the product or service.
- Conversions: How many users did what the marketer desired, such as purchasing a product, downloading content, or providing more information to the company (like their e-mail addresses).

Marketing Frameworks

Frameworks also assist in the use of digital tools and data. Marketers developed some of these frameworks well before digital tools were even conceived. Many of these frameworks have been used in nondigital, traditional industries, such as the food service, automobile, grocery, real estate, and financial services sectors for many years. The Wells Fargo Stagecoach in the late 1800s with the red paint and logo on the side is a great example of driving the *awareness* phase of the marketing funnel.

Customer Segmentation and Personas

Some companies make the mistake of ignoring the importance of knowing the customer, or they make the mistake of learning about individual current customers without a clear understanding of the desired customer. A recent example of the impact of not knowing the customer is the initial efforts by some health providers to encourage people to get the COVID-19 vaccine. When first made available, the strategic goal was to get the vaccine to the most vulnerable populations. Still, most of these providers required prospective patients to go to online portals to register to get the vaccine. The first target customers were older people. In many states, the target population was people 60 and older. Those target patients may have been less familiar with online portals through smartphones and computers than younger people. At least some of the target patients never had the chance to get a reservation because the providers didn't consider or understand how those target patients received information to convert them into vaccine recipients. Providers clearly defined the desired customer (people over 60), but access to reservations for those potential customers was through online reservation portals, which proved to be a challenge for many. Think about how many doctors, dentists, insurance agents, and other service providers have moved to predominantly online connections. It's critical for them to know how their customers and patients get information.

Understanding the broader customer type provides valuable information: where the customer gets information about products, how they like to purchase products, what resources they use to make decisions about buying a product, and what that particular customer set's needs are. Identifying different types of customers is called segmentation.

As an example, David worked with the owners of a small ice cream sandwich retail store for more than a year. He assisted the team with developing franchise plans. In the scope of that work, he also evaluated the store's marketing plan. The business offered two different types of services. One was the retail store, where customers could just drop in and buy a sandwich. The other was the catering business, where customers could be served at their desired location. These were distinct go-to-market approaches with discrete customer sets.

A simple way to evaluate this would be to say that two segments existed: retail customers and catering customers. As you can imagine, driving awareness, consideration, and conversion would vary from one customer segment to the other. The retail customer could just be walking by the store, see the signs and décor, and decide to come in. This is why store signage is critical for a retail business. On the other hand, a catering customer might learn about the store from an Internet search or word of mouth. Retail customers likely enter the store and buy an ice cream sandwich to eat themselves. Catering customers may be ordering for an office party, birthday party, or wedding—and might not even be consuming any of the product. Both segments represent different types of customers.

Inside each of these segments are different buyers, and they can be segmented further into personas, which are the character traits and motivations within each segment. Take an ice cream sandwich shop that is located near a university. There are several groups of customers in that "retail visit" segment: college students looking for a quick treat, a family coming by for a special dessert for the kids, and couples ending date night with an ice cream sandwich. If you think about these three subsegments, you can quickly identify some unique differences and begin to build personas for a prototypical customer.

The college student persona could be John, an undergrad in his early 20s, who is sensitive to price and the time it takes to get in and out of the store. He relies on Yelp reviews or recommendations from friends. He wants to get dessert from a place that is hip, trendy, and definitely Instagram worthy. Elizabeth, on the other hand, could represent a corporate event planner persona who gets information from event planning websites, tradeshows, or Internet searches. She is a 28- to 45-year-old professional interested in high-quality products that reflect her clients' tastes. She must meet their needs by providing on-time delivery, professional service, and good communication. Because quality is her most important criterion, she is not as sensitive to price as John. Elizabeth will pay more for a higher quality product and service.

Think about these two personas and any others you might create for the two segments. You'll quickly grasp the impact they each have on product definition, advertising, pricing, and customer needs. If the idea of value creation is to deliver a product or service that beats expectations, then it is critical that marketers actually know who the customer is and what they expect.

Four Ps of Marketing—The Marketing Mix

Edmund Jerome McCarthy introduced one of the most well-known and discussed frameworks in his 1960 book, *Basic Marketing: A Managerial Approach*, which was later popularized in marketing management textbooks by Philip Kotler. Kotler is frequently referred to as the "father of modern marketing." His 1967 book, *Marketing Management*, with Kevin Lane Keller, has been continuously updated and translated for use throughout the world.

The basic Four Ps approach is known as the "marketing mix." It focuses on four key areas.

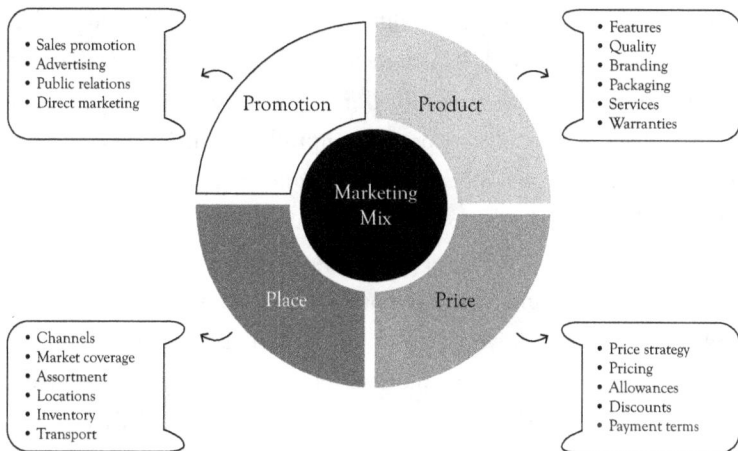

Figure 3.1 Four Ps of marketing—the marketing mix

Product refers to the actual deliverable that satisfies the customer's wants or needs, whether that be a physical product or a service. If you think back to the value equation and the idea of delivering something to a customer at an expected price, the first "P" stands for product. In the example of the ice cream sandwich shop, the store provides a dessert treat for customers.

For a walk-in customer, the desired product is an ice cream sandwich with warm cookies made to order. For a catering customer, the specific packaging and delivery might be a key component in the desired product, so the ice cream sandwiches are not gooey and messy by the time they reach the catering event. Understanding the wants and needs of a specific segment of customers helps identify the important product or service features that can differentiate your offerings from your competitors in that particular segment. People new to marketing often take for granted the mapping of product or service features to customer wants and needs. Yet it's an essential component of building a successful business. Including features that your customers don't care about results in extra costs that don't add value to the customer. Missing features that your customers do care about may result in lost sales.

Price refers to the cost the customer is required to pay in exchange for the product or service offered. Understanding what the customer is willing or able to pay for a product is complex and can be done in many ways. Different price strategies apply to different types of products and services. Price isn't always financial. It may include all elements of the customer's compensation, including time and effort.

The price that a volunteer pays a nonprofit, for instance, could be a financial donation, time, or lending their name to an outreach campaign. In the latter case, the price paid is reputational risk. Payment terms are also an essential facet of price. Requiring payment from the customer when they purchase and receive the product works fine for retail products purchased at a store. However, it would be a barrier for businesses buying computer systems, as corporate customers usually pay against an invoice with a specific time deliverable, usually within 30 days of delivery.

Placement is deciding where and how to sell your product or service. How a company delivers to the customer is a critical component of its value. Take the ice cream sandwich business. How a catering customer receives the product is different from how a retail customer receives it. A retail customer would come to the store to get their purchase as part of the overall experience. The catering customer would expect the product to be delivered directly to the event site. That customer may also expect the supplier to set up and manage the delivery of the product at the event.

To go one step further, the business could make several placement decisions that might impact customer satisfaction, pricing, and costs. Pre-packaging the sandwiches and selling them through grocery stores would introduce another step in the distribution process but could increase the number of sandwiches sold. It also could increase overall revenue. Selling through a grocery store isn't free. Profitability will be affected if the price cannot increase to cover the additional distribution costs, which is what the grocery store takes as its portion of the price.

One thing that may be a little confusing to people new to marketing is the use of the terms "channel" and "channel marketing." The companies that act as intermediaries to deliver your product or service to the end customer are called distribution or channel partners. They provide a channel to deliver your offering to the end customer.

If you were going to package ice cream sandwiches for distribution through grocery stores, you could go directly to a major grocery chain such as Albertsons, H-E-B, or even Walmart. If they agreed to carry your product, then they would be considered your "retail channel." The grocery store serves as the partner that delivers the final product to the end customer.

But let's say that you want the sandwiches to be sold at small and large stores throughout your region. Going to each store individually would be an expensive and time-consuming task. It would also take a variety of salespeople to be able to sell to both the large store chains and the small neighborhood stores. In that scenario, there are distribution companies, a.k.a. distribution partners, that specialize in distributing products to stores on behalf of manufacturers. This simplifies the purchase and logistics process for both the store people and the manufacturers. Each company that participates in the distribution of your product intends to make money on every sale. Essentially, they take a piece of the purchase transaction. The more partners that handle a product to deliver to the end customer, the more it costs the company in distribution fees. Those costs typically get passed on to the end user in price. While distribution partners can help drive more sales and get your product in front of more customers, this always comes at a cost. Placement has a significant impact on delivering and capturing value.

There are different types of channels in marketing. Distribution channels are how your product gets to the final customer. Communications or advertising channels are how you deliver your message to prospective customers. Service and support channels are the ways you provide after-sale support to existing customers. All channel types reach prospective, current, and existing customers.

Promotion refers to all of the activities that help prospective customers learn about your product or service offerings. Promotion's many facets include creating the promotion materials, identifying how the promotion material is presented to prospective customers, when that promotional material is presented, and how the promotions are measured for effectiveness. Advertising is a form of promotional material, but it is just one form. Trade shows, sponsorships, and social media content are all forms of promotional material.

With the advent of digital marketing tools during the past few years, there is more emphasis both on measuring the effectiveness of promotions and shaping advertising and promotion to the various marketing funnel stages. Those tools also track customers as they go through the purchasing process. Integrated promotion strategies that assist prospective customers through the phases of the cycle are referred to as nurturing. Promotional activities that build on another previous promotional activity are known as drip marketing or lead nurturing.

An example of drip marketing could be an e-mail that has interesting content or a link to a blog post or a web page. Marketers then may capture user information upon content engagement. Marketers then may send users more information over time to deepen engagement and connection with the prospective customer.

The Marketing Funnel

A common misconception is that all advertising and promotion is about "selling a product" and that a cool, catchy ad, or a clever campaign are all you need. In reality, many customers go through a lengthy process before deciding to purchase a product. This process is commonly referred to as the "purchase funnel." This funnel captures the customer journey from awareness of a product through to its purchase. Advertising executive Elias St. Elmo Lewis captured this process in 1898. He described the journey as awareness of a product that leads to interest in the product, resulting in desire for the product, and concludes with the purchase of the product. This is known as the Awareness, Interest, Desire, Action (AIDA) model. This model evolved as marketers became conscious of the benefits of customer loyalty and the value of positive references. Today, the different versions of the AIDA model are known as marketing funnels.

Good marketers use the marketing funnel framework to ensure that promotions drive customer behavior in a way desired by the business. The marketing funnel that we like to use is referenced at the beginning of this chapter. It has five stages:

- Awareness
- Consideration
- Conversion
- Loyalty
- Advocacy

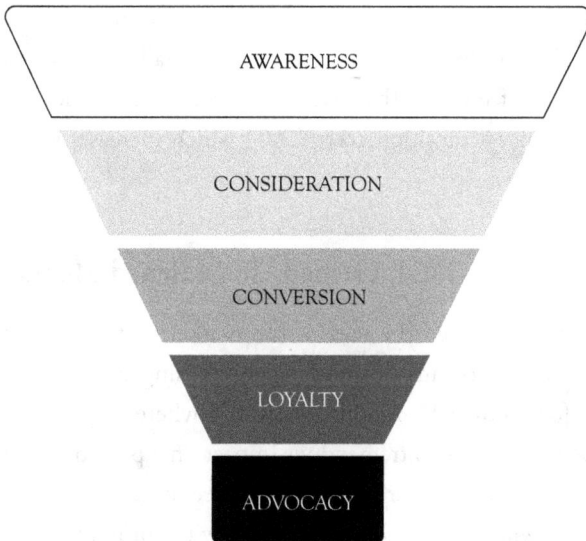

Figure 3.2 Marketing funnel

To make this simple, imagine the flow through the lens of a prospective customer. The marketer must alert the potential customer that the product exists (Awareness), encourage the prospect to consider acquiring or using the product (Consideration), and lead the customer to take any action that the company desires, such as purchasing the product, downloading an app, or providing an e-mail address (Conversion).

Many companies make the mistake of stopping there. But that's not the end of the customer's purchase journey. How the company interacts with the (now) customer after the purchase significantly affects the customer repurchasing from the company and buying more products (Loyalty). Companies that earn a high level of trust and loyalty have the opportunity to turn customers into references (Advocacy). Think about Apple or Tesla. Both of these companies are known for having a fanatical customer base that raves about their products. Apple's customers are so renowned for their advocacy that a quick Internet search will show that the terms "Apple Fanboy" or "Apple Fangirl" are commonly used to describe them. Talk to almost any Tesla owner, and you will likely hear gushing positives about their experience and the value of owning a Tesla car.

Remember that an important component of the value equation is cost. If customers are speaking positively about your product or service, then they may actually help reduce what you spend on marketing. What now takes three or four calls to a prospect may fall to one or two based on good word of mouth. That reduced marketing and sales cost means a lower customer acquisition cost (CAC) which increases your profit—more on that later.

POEM—Paid, Owned, and Earned Media

Now that we've covered the idea of the marketing funnel, let's discuss the vast number of communication and advertising channels available to marketers for product promotion. How and where to place advertising and messaging can have a tremendous impact on a promotion's effectiveness in terms of the number of people who see the promotion, the number of people who take the action intended by the promotion, the overall promotion cost, and the public awareness of the brand.

POEM Channel Model

Reviews
Media coverage
Guest posts
Influencers (free)
Word of mouth
Ratings

EARNED

PAID

Pay per click
Display ads
Remarketing
Retargeting
Paid social
Native ads
Influencers (paid)
Print ads
Radio and TV
Outdoor billboards
Direct mail

(Your) Website
Blog
Profiles
E-mail
Social Pages
Prospect and contact list

OWNED

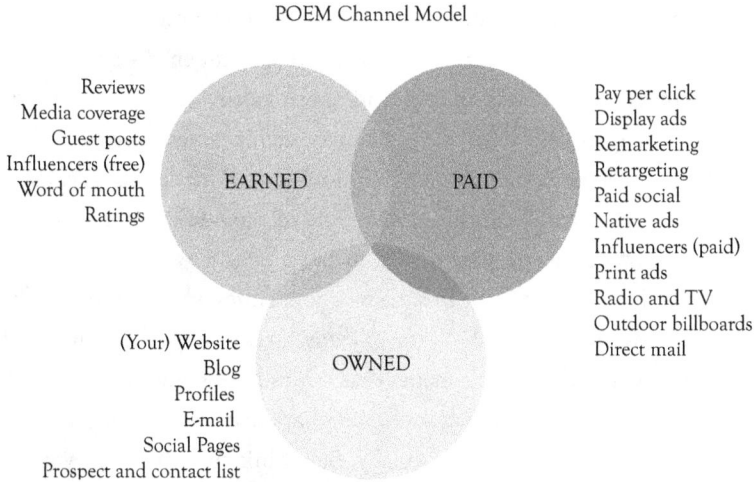

Figure 3.3 POEM marketing

Paid media refers to advertising channels that you pay to promote your product. A newspaper, television, or radio ad is an example of paid advertising. An outdoor billboard or direct mail campaign through the postal service are also examples of traditional paid channels. In the digital world, Google Display ads, Meta ads, YouTube sponsored videos, and other online platforms where you can pay for exposure are considered paid media. If you have to pay to get your messaging and promotion in front of prospective customers, then it is considered a paid channel.

Owned media refers to your company's website, Facebook page, YouTube channel, Instagram page, and other digital presences where you maintain the content and do not pay to post regularly. Your list of customer and prospect e-mails is also considered "owned" because you don't have to pay to send e-mails to that list. The value of owned media is that you control how much and how often you provide content of interest to your audience. The challenge with owned media is that it takes time to build traffic to those sites. It can take a while to get regular followers of your social media accounts and webpages organically, without advertising. It's common to use paid media initially to drive traffic to your owned media pages with the goal of reducing the need for paid traffic over time.

Earned media is the promotion you receive from third parties that helps advertise your product. Reviews by news media, news stories about your business, ratings on sites, and coverage of your product by bloggers are all examples of earned media. Social media influencers also can be sources of earned media if they provide positive coverage of your product on their own. But if you pay them to reference your product, they should be considered paid media. Word-of-mouth marketing is considered earned media. Encouraging customers to provide reviews on major sites is one way to get positive earned media.

If you doubt the value of this, think about times when you have considered going to a movie. Do you pay any attention to the number of stars a movie receives or comments that critics have made? Do you look up the movie on Rotten Tomatoes to see what critics and moviegoers say? You may say that you don't personally, but think about it when you do an online search. What generally shows up at the top of the searches? The first thing you see is usually the most commented-on or reviewed items. Research shows that consumers trust feedback and word of mouth more than they trust paid media.

Many companies make the common mistake of spending too much money on advertising through paid media. They are often disappointed with the results. One reason is that paid media, owned media, and earned media are all critical to a marketing plan. Think about your last purchase of a car. We bet that you saw an ad (paid media) somewhere that made you *aware* of the vehicle and encouraged you to *consider* buying it. Then, you probably searched for reviews of the car and looked at the articles written by auto experts and the comments by owners (earned media). Then you went to the website (owned media) of the car company to get more information about the vehicle, such as specifications, colors, and mileage. It would be a waste of money for a car company to invest in ads about their new car and have no reviews, or only bad reviews, on the car sites. Worse would be to pay money for advertising and then have prospects go to your website to find a poor layout, minimal information, or complicated navigation.

Why does this matter? Think about the value equation. How much money does it cost to run multiple ads to get a customer interested in your product? The more that you can reduce the overall cost of getting a customer to purchase your product or service, the more profit you have. The smart strategy is to ensure that all your owned media presences look good, work correctly, and have good content before you spend a penny on paid media. Next, smart marketers work on getting earned media through press reviews, customer feedback, and social media ratings. This is why experienced restaurateurs host "soft openings." Finally, when you know that the owned and earned media are working, then you spend money on paid media to accelerate the activity.

Porter's Five Forces

Another essential framework to understand in marketing identifies the forces that affect profitability. Michael Porter, a leading marketing expert at Harvard University, developed the Five Forces framework for evaluating the pressures on profitability.

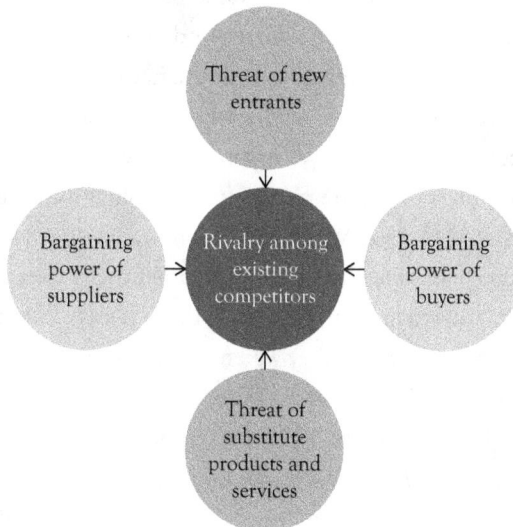

Threat of new entrants

Bargaining power of suppliers

Rivalry among existing competitors

Bargaining power of buyers

Threat of substitute products and services

Figure 3.4 Porter's five forces

Industry Rivals: These are your direct competitors who are selling similar products or services. The more competitors you have providing a similar offering, the more pressure is put on pricing. Convincing customers of the benefits of your product or service over the competition takes advertising, selling, and maybe even discounting to compete, which can drive up your costs and may require the lowering of price. That ultimately affects profitability.

Threat of Substitutes: Some other products or services can be used instead of your product. The threat of substitutes creates additional competition for your offering, even if it's not directly competing. For example, a motorcycle is a substitute for a car. While it doesn't directly compete, the motorcycle offers the user an alternative form of transportation at a lower price. In the same way, using an Internet search to get a legal document, like a template for a will, is a substitute for paying a lawyer to prepare a will. It's cheaper, even free—even if the completeness or appropriateness of these are open to debate. A lawyer who develops wills as part of their practice would be wise to identify other services that should be done, so charging for the will preparation could compete more effectively against the free option. Arguing the quality of the lawyer-developed will compared to the free downloaded will might be technically correct. But that isn't compelling enough for many potential clients to switch. More work in conveying the value of having a lawyer-prepared will, as well as the ancillary documents and services that the firm can provide, is an example of competing with the free substitute.

Threat of New Entrants: Fewer competitors in a market space—or a market space with a high level of profitability—will encourage new entrants that put pressure on pricing and profitability. Think about the market for cell phones. When the iPhone came out, no competitor offered the same level of features. But soon, other companies began introducing smartphones that competed with the iPhone. They still weren't direct competitors, though, as they weren't selling the same product. Only Apple sold iPhones. Then Google released Android. Smartphone manufacturers had direct competitors. Other phones did the same thing for customers, such as taking calls and running applications. Suddenly new entrants were in the space. The result? Phone manufacturers offered more discounting (less profit) and new, lower-priced iPhone models to compete. New entrants put pressure on profitability by introducing competition.

Supplier Power: The power of a supplier on your costs is higher when your product or service is dependent on unique materials or people with special skills. This power can have an impact on profitability because it increases costs. The general rule is that if there are few suppliers for a product, then the supplier has all of the power. They can charge whatever they want. Conversely, if there is a large number of suppliers, then the purchaser has all the power because they have multiple sources from which to choose. The COVID-19 pandemic brought awareness of the impact of supplier power. When the supply of materials became more limited due to the pandemic's impact on factory labor and persistent supply chain snarls, companies had only two choices: raise prices to absorb the increasing costs of materials or maintain price levels that could cause a reduction in profits.

Buyer Power: Similar to supplier power, if there are a small number of buyers, then the buyers have all of the power. But if there is a large number of buyers, then the seller has the power. You can see this in real estate. Suppose there are many properties on the market and few buyers. In that case, a buyer can demand a lower price for a property because there is so much competition for that buyer's purchase. On the other hand, if there are many buyers interested in a property, then the seller has the negotiating power and may be able to get more than the original asking price. Think about the home real estate market in 2021 and most of 2022. Many cities had more buyers than available houses for sale. It was common for buyers to bid many thousands of dollars over the asking price to win the bid to purchase a home.

Competitive Analysis

In addition to Porter's Five Forces, marketers must understand where their products and brands stand relative to market competitors. Customers always have a choice. It's a fallacy to think that your company or product is the only one that can satisfy a customer's needs.

As we discussed in the Five Forces, customers have alternatives even if they are neither cost-effective nor in the same product or service category. It's critical to understand where your product is relative to other offerings, regardless of whether you have direct competitors. Understanding the position of your product through the eyes of the customer helps you develop the messaging, advertising, and components of the Four Ps to be more attractive to prospective customers when compared with your competition.

There are two primary ways to conduct a competitive analysis:

- Look at your strengths and weaknesses at the company level when compared with your competition.
- Compare your product or service at the level of product features, price, and placement.

Here is a competitive analysis chart comparing a grocery store with other stores in the area.

	Our Store	Chain Competitor #1 (0.6 miles away)	Independent Competitor (1.8 miles away)	Chain Competitor #2—Superstore (1.1 miles away)	Quick Shop Store (0.4 miles away)
Size of Store	24,000 sq. ft.	35,000 sq. ft.	30,000 sq. ft.	52,000 sq. ft.	4,000 sq. ft.
Product Selection	Medium	High	Medium	Medium/Low (grocery brand options)	Low
Average Number of Checkout Lines/Store	4	8	4	18	2
In-Store Pharmacy	No	Yes	No	Yes	No
In-Store Bakery	Yes	Yes	No	Yes	No
Prepared Food Selection	Medium—chicken wing bar, prepacked cold options	Medium/High—roast poultry, chicken wing bar, salad bar, prepacked cold options	Small—prepacked cold options	In-store fast food vendor	High—Large selection of grab and go hot/cold food options
Personal Services (check cashing, money orders, utility bill payments, tax and licensing payments)	Check-cashing, money orders	All services	Check-cashing only	All services	All services
Cleanliness of Store (10 = most clean, 1 = least clean)	7	8	5	6	4
Price Position (10 = most competitive, 1 = least competitive)	5	6	5	8	3
Unique Offerings	Personal service, fresh produce and meat cut to order	Chain brand, product selection	Convenience, local ownership	Breadth of overall product selection options beyond groceries	Convenience

Figure 3.5 *Grocery store competitive analysis chart*

As you can see, it's a straightforward, realistic assessment comparing the marketer's store ("Our Store" in the table) with other stores in the market. What you can see from the chart is that our store is not a clear leader in a few of the categories. Personal service is the unique value proposition and is an option for focused messaging and marketing.

In Chapter 7, we will dig deeper into competitive analysis and positioning using Porter's Five Forces, the SWOT (strengths, weaknesses, opportunities, threats) framework, and feature comparison maps. Understanding these frameworks will help provide a baseline of the levers to use in successful marketing as we move into execution with the Strategic Marketing Framework.

Key takeaways from this chapter:

1. The marketing funnel illustrates the various stages of a customer's journey: before, during, and after the purchase of a product or service.
2. Customer segmentation refers to the process of categorizing customers based on shared characteristics.
3. The Four Ps of marketing, also known as the "Marketing Mix," is a fundamental marketing strategy framework that includes Product, Price, Promotion, and Placement.
4. POEM is an acronym for Paid, Owned, and Earned Marketing Channels. The model represents the different communication channels available to engage with prospective and current customers.
5. Porter's Five Forces analysis is a tool that assists in identifying the potential profitability pressures within your business model.

CHAPTER 4

Introducing the Strategic Marketing Framework

It might not be obvious how all these fundamental marketing frameworks relate to one another. In this chapter, we'll introduce an approach to bringing these elements together using a strategic marketing planning worksheet.

Think of this as a sort of "meta framework" that helps you put the results of your marketing assumptions and planning into a structure that will help you conceptualize the marketing plan. More than just identifying the target customer, it's also about determining the product or service and ultimately setting measures for success.

It has become a common practice to move strategic planning into a visual structure, easy for both top executives and entry-level employees to understand. People seem to grasp concepts and how they are connected to one another much more quickly in a visual framework. These frameworks provide simple models as the basis for deeper concepts and strategies to evolve.

An example of this type of framework is the Business Model Canvas, which helps entrepreneurs and startup teams brainstorm and visualize the critical elements and activities needed for a new business. Like the Business Model Canvas, we introduce the Strategic Marketing Framework as a tool to help with the initial planning and development of an effective and strategic marketing plan.

For marketing execution to be effective, some common concepts must be interconnected. To simplify and enhance the planning of these concepts, the Strategic Marketing Framework is designed to provide a broad visualization of the elements anticipated for driving a winning marketing strategy.

The person responsible for developing an integrated strategic marketing plan will find the framework useful. It allows for plans that focus on either a single product or service or multiple products and services—even products and services with distinctly different market applications.

Throughout this book, we will introduce sections of the framework as we cover different marketing topics. We recommend you to build your own Strategic Marketing Framework for your product or service as you move through the chapters. You may use this framework when building a business, brand, product, or marketing plan. You will learn more about these distinctions later in the book.

In the meantime, allow us to introduce the Strategic Marketing Framework.

This framework captures many important elements of various strategic marketing concepts in one worksheet.

The upper portion of the framework allows the marketer to think through and test the assumptions around the customer, product or service, and competition. It provides a way for you to specify, manage, and tune the longer-term strategic marketing decisions required to ensure your company's offerings are the most competitive for the target audience.

These internal activities are some of the upstream marketing elements that we introduced in Chapter 1. They determine who the target customer is, specify the features of the product or service to be developed and offered to the customer, and identify the competition. The lower portion of the framework comprises the downstream section of the marketing planning process.

The Strategic Marketing Framework should be a little more intuitive to understand the foundational marketing frameworks. For example, customer segmentation and the marketing funnel introduced in Chapter 3 can help in constructing your own framework and strategic marketing plan for your product, service, or brand. The traditional Four Ps of marketing are integrated into the Strategic Marketing

SEGMENT/ PRODUCT LINE Specify targets	LINE 1		LINE 2		U
PEOPLE Identify and describe those you're targeting	USER	CUSTOMER	USER	CUSTOMER	P S
PRODUCT/ FEATURES Identify key products or features for users and customers					T R E A M
STRATEGIC MARKETING GOALS What are you try-ing to achieve?					
COMPETITION Who are you up against?					
PRICE POSITION Ideal position vs. competition or price strategy					
KEY MESSAGES What matters to users/customers					D O
PROMOTIONS/ CAMPAIGNS Get creative					W N S
PLACEMENT Where you will run campaigns	DIGITAL	TRADITIONAL	DIGITAL	TRADITIONAL	T R
SUCCESS MEASURES How you will measure progress					E A M
NOTES					

Figure 4.1 Strategic Marketing Framework

Framework and appear in the People, Product, Pricing Position, and Promotion rows of the Strategic Marketing Framework.

All these framework elements should also help you develop strong key messages to position your product as a better choice relative to your competition.

The Strategic Marketing Framework works because it requires you, as a marketing strategy planner, to think through and identify what success will look like and how it should be measured during the strategic planning process. This prompts you to evaluate each of the framework's elements and consider whether they will lead to meeting the marketing team's measures of success. This element will also help the marketing team identify the metrics that will show whether the strategic marketing plans are delivering.

We did not create these marketing models, paradigms, or planning components. They are longstanding elements of marketing. Many resources and books exist to assist you in understanding each of the specific components more fully and to further develop your skills as a strategic marketer. For example, there are a number of books and online training materials available regarding customer segmentation or pricing methods. Once you've begun to execute your strategic marketing plan and identify opportunities for improving the model, you likely will understand the areas where you want to go deeper. You also will have a better understanding of where you need more help and resources.

We hope that this book may also help you become better and more aware of your needs when you are hiring marketing team members, marketing consultants, advertising agencies, and marketing service providers.

In the following chapters, we will provide more detail to broaden your understanding of the Strategic Marketing Framework and help you build your own strategic marketing plan.

Key takeaways from this chapter:

1. The Strategic Marketing Framework Worksheet is a tool designed to facilitate the visualization and organization of your marketing strategy as you develop it.
2. The worksheet is divided into Upstream and Downstream marketing sections.
3. Throughout the strategic planning process, revisiting and revising previous sections is common as new marketing insights and information emerge.

CHAPTER 5

Identifying the Product and Service Offerings

One of the first things to do when putting together a strategic marketing plan is to separate your company's offerings into distinct business or product lines. Most companies have multiple product or service offerings that appeal to different types of customers.

This helps identify the first elements of your Strategic Marketing Framework. The top of the framework is where the focus of the marketing activities is designed to drive sales and revenue. A marketing strategy can encourage company (or brand) awareness, drive product sales, or reach a specific target segment of the business. As we start building the strategy, the focus of the marketing activities will be put in the top box(es) of the Strategic Marketing Framework.

SEGMENT/PRODUCT LINE Specify targets	LINE 1	LINE 2

Figure 5.1 Target segment/product focus block

Using our earlier example, an ice cream shop might have two business lines that generate revenue. Each line is based on the same general product—ice cream—but they are distinct sources of revenue.

As discussed earlier, one line of revenue may come from a retail consumer business in the form of an ice cream storefront that sells to individuals. The other line could come from providing ice cream products as a commercial catering business. The two likely have significantly different customers. Each group will have different needs, different expectations around price, and different ways to obtain information.

If the store just offered a single product line and tried to price and market to both audiences in a similar fashion, then the store would fail to optimize the amount of money earned on the transactions. Another potential pitfall: the shop could fail to be competitive with other players in its market. For example, if the company sold an ice cream cone at the store for $4, that price wouldn't be unreasonable for a walk-in retail customer. But if you were going to set up ice cream catering with the price being the same, and you were delivering 50 premade cones, suddenly, that $200 for a dessert might not be attractive to a catering customer.

Think about Ben and Jerry's ice cream business. The stores are located throughout the United States. Ben and Jerry also have prepacked ice cream available in retail grocery stores, most commonly in one-pint containers. Each approach serves a different customer need, offers the product in a different delivery mode, and is promoted differently.

Let's discuss our earlier grocery store example. Grocery stores have multiple product lines, such as dry goods, produce, meat, fish, poultry, and baked goods. They could build a strategy around each of these individually, or they could group them by product, such as fresh food and packaged goods. If they were to focus on fresh foods as a target product group, it would be easy to see elements that could be built around items such as fresh meat, fresh produce, and freshly baked bread. As you read this, you may think about some of your local grocery stores and how they market or highlight their fresh food offerings.

This is why it is so important to start by closely examining the overall business and attempting to understand different business or product lines offered to customers. Identifying the specific business segments allows for the optimization of all of the activities in marketing. That helps in identifying the product and service features desired by customers in each segment and targeting the messaging and marketing investment you make.

Here are four examples of how to apply this diversification of product or business lines to the Strategic Marketing Framework. We'll use two examples for each company.

The first business example would be a taco food trailer, which is very much like the ice cream shop. Both might have a walk-up retail business and a catering business for commercial customers.

The food trailer proprietor must target customers and set the pricing and promotion differently than the catering business. These two business lines may not be priced or promoted the same way.

SEGMENT/ PRODUCT LINE Specify targets	LINE 1 Taco Trailer Walkup Business	LINE 2 Delivery services (i.e., Doordash, Uber Eats)

Figure 5.2 Segment target example for taco trailer business

Let's now consider how an accounting consulting firm might approach business line segmentation. By its very nature, this type of company likely has at least two separate business lines. The first would offer tax preparation services to individuals. The second would target small- and mid-sized businesses that want bookkeeping, financial planning, and other services beyond annual tax filings. These distinct business segments in the same company represent different target customers, different pricing, different needs, and different ways to reach those customers. In this example, you may have state and federal tax return preparation requirements, which would be one set of products going through the same types of customers. The tax preparation for an individual may be priced at an hourly rate, while the small- and mid-sized business accounting practice could be priced as a monthly fee for all services, including tax preparation. These two different business lines will have different sets of target customers. While the final bill paid will vary to a large degree between the two customer types, pricing is developed and optimized for the specific segment.

SEGMENT/ PRODUCT LINE Specify targets	LINE 1 Business Customers (bookkeeping and tax)	LINE 2 Individual Tax Preparation

Figure 5.3 Segment target example for accounting business

The tax preparation firm is clearly a service business. The taco trailer is unique in that it could be considered either a service business or a product business, depending on whether the marketing efforts are based on the product itself or on the convenience of the food service. Companies that focus mainly on product offerings require the same segmentation approach as service providers. Take a laptop computer company as an example. One business line could serve corporate customers, while another could cater to individual consumers.

The laptops offered in both business lines possess many of the same components: a processor, memory, hard drive storage, a keyboard, and a network connection. The differentiation between the products appears in characteristics including screen size, thickness, and weight.

The differences optimize the product for the specific needs of those within each target customer segment. People who frequently travel may desire the lightest and thinnest computers for ease of transport and storage. People who use their laptop computers primarily on their desktops generally desire large screens, lots of hard drive storage, and larger keyboards.

Another example would be a bike manufacturer that creates segments based on the customer type.

SEGMENT/ PRODUCT LINE Specify targets	LINE 1 Mountain Bikes	LINE 2 Road Bikes

Figure 5.4 Segment target example for bicycle business

While both of these products are bikes, the separate business segments serve two distinct customers: mountain bikers and road cyclists. Bike features will depend on rider usage. The weight of the front forks on a road bike would likely be more important to a road cyclist, while the ability of the front forks and shocks on a mountain bike to withstand hitting logs, rocks, and holes could be a priority for a mountain biker.

A range of bikes may exist for customers identified as mountain bikers or road cyclists. Mountain bikes represent one business line for one type of customer. Road bikes would be another business line for a different type of customer.

The bike store will need to disseminate information using different channels to reach each type of customer because the two groups likely obtain bike information from different sources.

Mountain bikers, for instance, go to different online sites and read different magazines than road cyclists do. The magazines *Mountain Flyer* and *Mountain Bike Action Magazine* are frequently read by mountain bikers, while *Road Bike Action* magazine and *Bicycling* are targeted at road cyclists.

The business owner also will apply different pricing to the two lines. The products offered for mountain biking grouped together would be called the Mountain Bike product portfolio. The portfolio would have the bikes, the components for the bikes, and the accessories for mountain bikers. The portfolio would include different types of tires, chains, and handlebars, among other features. All of those items are part of the product portfolio. The Road Bike product portfolio would be similar in organization. It would include road bikes with specific road bike features such as specialized front forks, suspensions, handlebars, and wheels.

The customers' expectations of pricing, where customers go to obtain bike information, and the competitors offering similar products are important and sometimes different depending on the type of bike and customer segment.

Additionally, within each of these companies' business or product lines, the offerings usually are priced unique to that respective offering and set of customers. You can't charge $10,000 to one person and $500 to another. Well, technically, you can, but it's likely customer satisfaction will be very low for the $10,000 customer if they got the exact same product or service as the $500 customer.

The segmentation also directly affects how and where you deliver information—"messaging" in marketing parlance—to potential customers about your offerings. The target customers of the business accounting services are likely business owners or managers. These customers probably get their information through the same channels. This is where being a member of the local chamber of commerce may be important because that provides a forum to meet those leaders. Additionally, the prospective customers of this group are going to have certain expectations regarding accounting services. As a result, your hourly rates for your small- and mid-sized customers will differ from those for your individual customers.

All these examples should demonstrate why it is crucial to separate the distinct business lines in your framework worksheet.

This business segmenting happens even in large enterprise customer companies. For example, while David worked for Dell Technologies Inc. (NYSE: DELL) during the 1990s, when it was known as Dell Computer Corporation, two notebook lines existed: Latitude and Inspiron.

Dell managed both notebooks within one business unit, but the company developed and marketed each of them for different customers. Dell priced them differently, advertised each of them differently, and sold them through different internal distribution channels. The Inspiron notebook line targeted individual consumers. Dell advertised the product through direct mail, the Dell website, consumer publications, and television ads. The company targeted the Latitude laptop line to corporate customers with a direct sales force calling on buyers at the prospective customer sites.

Laptop components are always changing. New and better components come at a rapid pace from suppliers. Managing products with a high level of change is always challenging. Retail customers almost always want the latest, fastest, and newest features in their laptop purchases. Corporate customers typically want specific models of laptops to be available to their employees for much longer than their components are available from suppliers.

Because of this diversity of needs, Dell maintained Latitude components and configurations longer than many competitors that also made laptops for commercial customers to ensure that they could fulfill the needs of the corporate customers. Corporate customers were willing to pay a different price compared to the consumer laptops for the Latitude line. It simplified the management of large batches of laptops when they could have the same or very similar configurations. Dell advertised the Latitude products in business publications. In addition, the segmentation allowed Dell to add features to the Latitude products that were desired and specific to business users.

It is important to understand that a product line or business line is different from a brand name. A brand is a name and associated iconography that is assigned to products or services to help distinguish them from other products or services. A product line is a set of products that are related to the brand name. Companies can have multiple brands as well as multiple product lines within the brand. Consider Apple's offerings. They have MacBooks, iPads, and iPhones. All three are brand names. Within the iPad brand, multiple product lines exist: the iPad, the iPad Pro, the iPad Mini, and the iPad Air. Apple developed the different brands to identify the products within those product lines as different from other products.

Multiple product lines or individual products within the same category of offerings are called "product portfolio." You see this often in businesses where you have a set type of products for a specific customer group. If you have ever been to a mobile phone store, then you've likely seen this with the iPhone. Many stores carry the different iPhone lines: iPhone 11, iPhone 12, and iPhone 13, for instance. Each of these lines also has products specific to a user segment: iPhone 12, iPhone Pro Max, and iPhone 12 Mini, for example. Different iPhone lines also boast accessories specific to each line. If you look closely at an iPhone 12 and an iPhone 13, the differences become apparent. For example, the iPhone 13 has a faster processor than the iPhone 12. Apple creates unique product line names to differentiate between the products. The discipline of administering all of these products is known as portfolio management.

If you are planning on using the Strategic Marketing Framework worksheet for your business, this is where you can start. In the uppermost part of the worksheet, under the "Product/Business Line" label, you should identify your business's product portfolio, line of business, or product line. If your business involves multiple products or areas requiring distinct strategies, you may need to use several sheets. However, it is recommended to begin by focusing on just one or two segments.

As discussed in previous chapters, the value equation demonstrates that strong marketing means delivering value to the customers in exchange for capturing value for the company. If you are ineffectively marketing your products and you are spending too much, or your customer acquisition costs are too high, you are not effectively and efficiently capturing value.

Understanding and segmenting the business lines is a critical task as we move into the next phase of strategic marketing planning. In Chapter 6, we will identify the target customers for each of these unique offerings.

Key takeaways from this chapter:

1. It is not unusual for businesses to maintain similar product lines or services that cater to distinct customer segments. For instance, a tax accounting firm may provide tax services to both individuals and corporate clients.

(*Continues*)

(Continued)

2. Tailoring marketing efforts for each specific offering enables optimizing features, messaging, pricing, and competitive analysis.

3. The term "product portfolio" is commonly used to describe an array of products or services. Companies that excel in marketing fine-tune their strategies for every offering within the portfolio.

CHAPTER 6

Understanding Customers and Segments

To put a strategy together for a product or a set of business lines, understanding the customer for these different offerings is essential. In this chapter, we'll share ways to identify and segment your target customers. These approaches are critical to ensuring that you deliver the desired product at the right price through the proper messaging channels to reach the respective target customers.

As we pointed out in Chapter 2, it's crucial to understand the difference between a product user and a product buyer. Both could be customers, but the product marketer must be aware that each has different attributes and interests.

Let's say you're targeting a consulting firm. The user of your product may be an employee of the firm. However, the buyer of your product may be the firm's chief executive officer or its chief financial officer. The buyer approves or pays for the purchase. The buyer is the decision maker. The user is the person who does something with the product or works with the service. In many cases, these are the same person, but it's not uncommon in business-to-business transactions to have these be different people.

They may be members of the same segment, but inside that customer group, a buyer and a user are different.

Let's look at a fast-food business. In this case, the actual consumer (user) of the product may be a child asking the parent (buyer) to get a burger. The customer, on the other hand, is the parent.

Even though the target customer *segment* may be families, the messaging for the child (user) could be different than for the parent (buyer).

Customer Segmentation

The initial step in segmentation is to look at your current customers or target customers and attempt to group them. Is there a commonality among the demographics within this group? Can you separate female buyers from male buyers, or, for example, is there a clustering of women younger than 21 versus men older than 21? Can you delineate distinct groups who might behave or appear to be different from one another?

The price that a prospective set of customers is willing or able to pay for a product also can inform how you approach your marketing strategy.

These customer groups are known in marketing as "customer segments." This activity is called "customer segmentation."

Customers can be segmented different ways but often fall into four primary groups:

- Demographic: by variables such as age, gender, marital status, or family status
- Psychographic: by psychological characteristics such as beliefs, values, social groups, interests, relationship status, price sensitivity, or lifestyles
- Behavioral: by how they make their buying decisions such as benefits sought, how they engage with your business— e-commerce versus buying items at a brick-and-mortar store, for instance—product usage, and customer loyalty, otherwise known as "repurchase behavior"
- Geographic: by where they live based on countries, states, regions, cities, or neighborhoods to understand the needs of the customers in those areas

Imagine a homebuyer seeking a house that costs more than $1 million. Now imagine a first-time homebuyer whose budget or ability to qualify for a home loan requires a listing price of less than $200,000. A real estate agent who is marketing and showing homes priced above $1 million to a prospective customer who can't qualify for more than a $200,000 mortgage is not making good use of the prospective customers' time, their time, or the advertising dollars used to get the prospective customer.

Each buyer seeks different features. Each also will obtain home purchasing information differently. The person looking to buy the more expensive home likely will be looking at features such as square footage, make and quality of the appliances and fixtures, and design. The person seeking the first-time home likely will be more concerned about things like location, number of rooms, and an appraisal that meets home loan qualification requirements. A prospective buyer looking to purchase a higher-end, more expensive home may look for a real estate agent who advertises in publications targeted at wealthier readers or may rely on word-of-mouth marketing through referrals. A first-time buyer may call a local real estate office or visit open houses in the buyer's perceived price range. Knowing the prospective buyer and how they get information can help the real estate agent target the right prospect.

Here are some ways business owners could identify users and customers for different business lines or product segments.

SEGMENT/ PRODUCT LINE Specify targets	LINE 1 Taco Trailer Walkup Business		LINE 2 Delivery services (e.g., Doordash, Uber Eats)	
PEOPLE Identify and describe those you're targeting	USER Individuals Families Couples	CUSTOMER Person who pays for the tacos	USER Meeting attendees, event goers, etc.	CUSTOMER Person who selects and orders for the delivery

Figure 6.1 Customer identification example for taco trailer business

As with the ice cream shop example in the last chapter, a taco trailer company has two different business lines. One is the trailer that serves walk-up customers. The other is the catering business, where the taco trailer provides food to a location or for pickup to be served as part of an event. These two business lines differ. So do the respective users and customers. In this example, the user and customer in the food trailer walk-up business may be the same person with the same needs and wants.

On the catering side, the customer frequently is not a user. The customer might be an office administrator buying tacos for a lunch meeting or an event planner buying tacos for an event. The customer and user could have very different desires and expectations. For instance, a local university provides lunches for graduate students attending classes on Saturdays. As the buyer of the lunches, the administrator is looking for the widest variety of choices at the best prices since they are providing lunches for many students. From the users' perspective (the students being fed), the freshness and quality of the food, the presentation, and the taste are what matters. If they aren't happy with the purchase, the university administrator, as the buyer, definitely hears about it. The administrator's goals include selecting food vendors that offer a variety of good food choices, ensuring the food is delivered on time, and finding a reasonable price.

SEGMENT/ PRODUCT LINE Specify targets	LINE 1 Mountain Bikes		LINE 2 Road Bikes	
PEOPLE Identify and describe those you're targeting	USER Bike rider	CUSTOMER Bike rider or parent of younger bikers	USER Biker rider	CUSTOMER Bike rider or parent of younger bikers

Figure 6.2 Customer identification example for the bike business

The bike shop is a products business. The user and customer profiles are the same for both product types: the user is a bike rider and is also the buyer. Why do we care about separating these between the two product category columns if they are the same? While the user and customer profiles are the same, the product features, the wants and needs of the customers, and the price expectations likely vary for users of a road bike compared to those of a mountain bike.

The mountain bike rider may be more interested in a bike's ability to endure rugged terrain with minimal repairs. In contrast, the road bike rider may be more interested in speed, weight, and price. These customer segments have different needs and interests.

We can apply the same principles when looking at a service business, such as an accounting consulting firm. Many accountants provide year-long bookkeeping support to businesses and income tax preparation for individuals.

If you think about the relationships, the bookkeeping business is an ongoing engagement for the accounting firm. Individual tax preparation

SEGMENT/ PRODUCT LINE Specify targets	LINE 1 Business Customers (bookkeeping and tax)		LINE 2 Individual Tax Preparation	
PEOPLE Identify and describe those you're targeting	USER Executives, board members, tax authorities, lenders	CUSTOMER Person in charge of finance or accounting reporting	USER Individual, spouse (filing jointly, or family)	CUSTOMER Person responsible for the tax filings

Figure 6.3 Customer identification example for an accounting business

is more of a transactional business that occurs once a year when income tax season rolls around. These separate business lines represent customers and users with unique needs that are specific to the type of customer or user segment.

The likelihood of an individual tax preparation customer switching to another tax preparation firm is much higher than a business customer with ongoing, monthly activities that build a stronger relationship between the customer and the accounting firm. The costs of switching to another accounting firm are much higher for a business customer than for an individual tax preparation customer. The time it would take to bring a new firm up to speed on the bookkeeping processes is potentially a high cost all by itself.

Knowing who the users and buyers of your product or service are allows you to monitor sales to those customers and see which segment is growing or shrinking within your customer base. Understanding who they are and what is happening in terms of purchase activity allows you to adjust your messaging, product, or pricing approach as needed to appeal to those segments. Your goal should be to add and keep your customers. Losing customers is known as "customer turnover."

Common business terms you may hear used when discussing customer turnover are "retention rate," "churn rate," and "attrition rate." Retention rate represents customers who stay and continue to be active customers of the company. The churn rate is the number or percentage of customers who leave the company in a short period of time. Attrition rate refers to customers who stop being customers during a specific period of time.

This is crucial: It's much more expensive to acquire a new customer than it is to keep an existing customer. From the value equation standpoint, the higher your retention rate and the lower your churn or attrition rate, the more value the company receives because you have to spend less on marketing to drive revenue.

A term used in marketing directly related to this is the customer lifetime value (CLV). The longer you can keep an existing customer, the higher your CLV likely is. It is calculated by multiplying the estimated average transaction size (AVG) by the number of purchases (PURCH) in a year by the average purchasing lifetime (YEARS) of a customer. CLV is calculated as:

$$AVG \times PURCH \times YEARS = CLV$$

If the average transaction of a McDonald's purchase is $10, for example, and a customer visits every three weeks on average, or 17 times a year, then the average annual customer value is $170. If McDonald's retains a customer for 30 years, then the CLV for that customer is $5,100. McDonald's spent almost $655 million in worldwide advertising in 2020. That is a lot of money to spend to attract a customer who comes in once or twice and ultimately decides not to return. The CLV for that customer will be very low. McDonald's, like most businesses, wants to build a long-term relationship with its customers.

From a marketing strategy standpoint, identifying the differences in retention between individual and business customers may lead the accounting firm to create new services for its individual tax customers. Those services would aim to keep them engaged throughout the year and, possibly, create new revenue streams. Leading tax preparation firm, Kansas City-headquartered H&R Block, has mastered this. One of its oft-used taglines is "Block has your back." The firm also has a service called Block Advisors that provides bookkeeping and business services throughout the year.

The company has added new services, such as a mobile app that assists in keeping up with filing requirements. The app also includes tax calculators and services that allow customers to get advance payments for future refunds.

Identifying the needs and wants of users and customers is critical in building out the strategic plan for a service business. But this type of approach isn't unique to service businesses. Think about your local grocery store. Many grocery chains have introduced loyalty cards and mobile applications. The loyalty tools provide special discounts on products when in the store. More importantly, they provide opportunities for the grocery chain to communicate with customers through weekly digital ads and coupons. Some of these mobile apps store previous purchases, which makes it easier for customers to recreate their shopping preferences. That enables the store to stay engaged with the customer. It also provides the grocery store with user information so they can understand users by segment. Store executives can analyze purchase data from the loyalty app by segment wants and interests. Most major chains, such as Whole Foods, Stop & Shop, Smith's Food and Drug, Albertsons, and Safeway, now have mobile loyalty apps.

Once you have identified the customers and users for each business segment, you will want to understand these groups to ensure that the marketing strategy is tuned to deliver value to these groups. Lack of specificity often leads to generic messaging and unnecessary features that result in higher costs or products that claim to do everything for everybody but ultimately appeal to only a few. In order to target the pricing, product features, messaging, and distribution, it is useful to segment customers and target specific customer groups, just as we have throughout this book for product and business lines.

Organizations need to understand the available market segments and their respective sizes so that they can set companywide goals. The same understanding may be valuable to a small- or mid-sized business that's building a strategic plan.

Still, at this point in strategy development, it's useful to identify the users and customers at a broader and general level. Later, as you begin to implement the strategic plan, you may find it beneficial to go deeper into sizing and researching the segments to further improve your execution. But at this point, what we've identified is more than enough to move forward in developing the strategic framework.

Whether you are using a simple identification of users and customers or a more detailed customer segmentation, when delineating segments, you should be sure that the groups are clearly different from one another. A corporate buyer differs from a consumer buyer and represents a clear segment of the market. A buyer who is younger than 25 and a buyer who is older than 25 are mutually exclusive. The same buyer can't be older than 25 and younger than 25 simultaneously. Local buyers versus long-distance buyers are another example of mutually exclusive segmentation.

It's possible and common to mix different categories of segments. One segment could be consumers younger than 25 who live within five miles of the ice cream shop and prefer to order using mobile apps before arriving. That segment is identifiable, unique, and targetable with advertising and messaging. Another segment could be consumers younger than 25 who are visiting from another location.

When identifying segments, it's vital to ensure they are large enough to be meaningful. If the segment identified accounts for less than 10 percent of the total target customer base, you might need to rethink your segmentation. Typically, customer segmentation for a business or product line should be limited to not more than four or five segments. Developing too many segments makes it challenging to manage. Beyond that, smaller segments could cause business owners or executives to spend time and money on groups that may already be addressable in the other, more significant segments.

Marketers regularly use clearly defined names to identify segments. For example, the families who come into the ice cream shop and purchase with their children could be called "family buyers," while the corporate and wedding planners could be called "catering people." Family buyers and catering people would be understandable segments that you could communicate to other people.

Could you segment wedding planners and corporate catering planners into further additional segments? You could, and it might make sense if those segments are large enough to be significant and targetable. Otherwise, it's not worth it because too much time, energy, and money would be spent on something that would not yield a meaningful return on investment.

It's important to think about the segments in terms of their respective size, their exclusivity, and their targetability. You always want segments that are meaningful, targetable, and understandable.

The more we know about the individual segments, the more we can do research and learn the answers to the following questions:

- Where do buyers and customers get information about the products they purchase?
- What are the unique needs they have for the product or service you're offering?
- What price points are those customers willing to pay?
- Are they the actual buyer, or are they the user?

The more information we have about a segment, and the more clarity we have on those segment-customer needs and wants, the easier it is to build out the rest of your marketing framework and put together a successful marketing strategy.

Key takeaways from this chapter:

1. Understanding the unique traits of the customer segments for each product or service in the portfolio is essential.
2. Product user and product buyer are both customer types, and often they have different needs or wants.
3. Grouping customers with similar attributes is called "customer segmentation."
4. Customers can be segmented based on demographics, psychographics, geographic locations, or behavioral commonalities.
5. Customer retention is a key objective of marketing. CLV is a metric utilized to assess the long-term value of a retained customer.

CHAPTER 7

Understanding the Competition

One of the most important things that needs to be done early to build a strong marketing strategy is an analysis of your competitors. Once we have identified who the competitors are and could be, we need to find a way to lay out the competitive differences. We call this "characterizing the competition." This is not different from sports. If you want to win a game, the more you know and understand your competitors' strengths and weaknesses, the better you can plan to win.

Competitive analysis includes understanding the product offerings, marketing, customer segmentation, pricing strategies, and sales strategies of the companies competing for your customers.

We can't overstate the importance of understanding the competitive landscape in building a strong strategic marketing plan. If you don't understand how the competition is appealing to potential customers whom you want to attract, then you will have a tough time building a marketing strategy that will lure customers from competitors.

David led Dell's product marketing teams for both the notebook and workstation product groups from 1994 to 2000 before leaving to cofound and lead Motion Computing. When he and his colleagues developed the strategic efforts for the Dell laptop product line, they used a competitive analysis to build a robust marketing plan. The laptop marketing team examined the top competitors' product features, competitive positioning claims, typical price changes, and launch timings to help understand the competitive environment and the best and worst times to announce new products and product line changes. This insight and resulting marketing activities helped drive Dell's rapid market rise in the product categories. Understanding your competitors' marketing, pricing, and sales strategies allows you to organize your activities for maximum impact at the lowest cost.

The first task in completing a competitive analysis is to identify the companies competing for your potential customers.

Approach this exercise from a customer's perspective. Are they looking to buy a product or use a service that you offer? Where else could they go to purchase that product or service?

Thinking about the different paths to purchase a product will help you develop messaging, pricing, and advertising to reach your potential customers. Knowing who the competitors are and evaluating their approaches to attracting customers also will help you see opportunities and weak spots in your offerings.

The bike framework example we presented earlier demonstrates how to identify the potential competition for prospective customers. In that example, no need exists to differentiate between the user and the customer for competitors.

SEGMENT/ PRODUCT LINE Specify targets	LINE 1 Mountain Bikes		LINE 2 Road Bikes		
PEOPLE Identify and describe those you're targeting	USER Bike rider	CUSTOMER Bike rider or parent of younger bikers	USER Biker rider	CUSTOMER Bike rider or parent of younger bikers	
PRODUCT/ FEATURES Identify key products or features for users and customers					U P S T R E A M
STRATEGIC MARKETING GOALS What are you trying to achieve?					
COMPETITION Who are you up against?	Online (Amazon, eBay) Bikes R Us (within 20 mi) REI Academy Outdoors		Online (Amazon, eBay) Bikes R Us (within 20 mi) Walmart, Target, Academy Outdoors		

Figure 7.1 Bike offering framework competition example

You will notice that competition is not the next section to fill out in the framework worksheet. That's because we will use the analysis of the competition and its offerings to help identify the key features those prospective customers evaluate when making purchase decisions. Doing so also will help us set strategic marketing goals.

Product Competitiveness

Understanding how your product or service compares to those being offered by other companies is critical to successful marketing. These companies are your competitors. In general, there are two types of competitors: direct and indirect. Let's look at Papa John's, the pizza business. Companies such as Domino's Pizza and Pizza Hut are direct competitors. They have similar pizza products and offer similar ways to get their pizza—delivery, takeout, or in-store dining. But for someone who is considering pizza for a meal, casual-dining restaurants, such as BJ's Restaurant & Brewhouse or The Cheesecake Factory, which have pizzas on their menus as a choice, are also competitors. Ready-to-eat frozen pizzas available for purchase in grocery stores also could be considered competition. But they are indirect competitors. Strong marketing teams understand where their products compete, directly and indirectly, with other products on features, price, and customer expectations.

Evaluating the competitiveness of a specific product or service is done through a process called "feature analysis." In a feature analysis, you create a table of your products and your competition's products side by side. Put your product or service in the first column and list its features in order of importance to a customer segment. Then, rank where your product or service stacks up against the competition.

If we look at the ice cream sandwich offering as an example, one competitor could be another ice cream store. It also could be a donut store. Or it could be a fast-food restaurant. Let's compare Baskin-Robbins, McDonald's, and store-bought, packaged ice cream sandwiches.

Customers may want the opportunity to select toppings for their ice cream sandwiches. Do either Baskin-Robbins or McDonald's offer cookies and ice cream together? If the answer is yes, you need to identify which one does and identify where their offerings are better than yours and where they are not. How does your product stack up to the competition? Do they have toppings? Are the ice cream sandwiches large or small? How many cookie flavors do they have? How many ice cream flavors do they offer? What are the competition's prices for these various features and product options? These things may seem qualitative and based on loose assumptions, and in some cases, they are. The feature analysis is intended to compare the features or elements that are considered important decision points by customers and prospective customers. These elements would be components of the table that rank competitive products relative to yours.

You should evaluate these product features based on their appeal and importance to the target market segment. For example, evaluating the type of packaging that the sandwich comes in is probably of little value if your target market is a family looking for dessert after a meal out. But there are customers to whom packaging is important, such as environmentally conscious Generation Z consumers. Elements of an ice cream sandwich comparison that could be important to customers might include price, freshly baked cookies or prebaked cookies in the sandwiches, or the number of toppings offered.

Adding the price to your table will also help you understand the price positioning of your competitors. Who is your highest-priced competitor, and what do they offer that supports the premium price? Is there a way to use your lower price to attract customers? Or is there something that they are offering that you should consider adding to your offering? What do they have to offer that justifies being seen as the premium price competitor?

It will also allow you to see what products they are offering at a lower price. What trade-offs is the competition making to be able to set that price?

The higher-priced competitor could be charging for everyday things you have embedded in your pricing, such as warranty coverage or service guarantees. The lower-priced competitor might not be offering the features that you provide. Understanding how these products are lined up by features and competitors is a critical element of a good competitive analysis. Doing so will provide you with clear ideas of how best to position your product for your target customers in pricing, messaging, and product delivery.

Product Placement and Distribution

It's also important to understand how the competitors distribute their products. How do they make their products available for customers to purchase? Is it easier or more difficult than how you make your offerings available? Are there distributors or retailers that help sell and distribute their products? As discussed in an earlier chapter, the ways companies deliver products to customers are called distribution channels. The distribution channel can be a competitive advantage or disadvantage, depending on the customer relationship. Some will preclude you from selling your products to customers if a distributor or competitor has an exclusive relationship with your target customer. Or they could provide an advantage in reaching customers that exceed your reach.

If your business is an accounting firm or a real estate agency, are there potential clients you can't attract because they are loyal to another service firm? What are those firms? What are the reasons your competitors have an advantage that is preventing you from accessing the market?

Suppose your company sells a computer hardware product or consumer-packaged goods (CPG) product. CPG products are items that come in a box, bottle, bag, or another type of container. They include beverages, snacks, and canned goods. Do distribution barriers exist that enable your competitors to have an advantage? Is there some advantage you might exploit?

For example, if we wanted to package an ice cream sandwich to sell in grocery stores, is there a way we can persuade stores to accept our product? Or do we need to go through a distributor to get on the grocery store shelf?

It's essential to determine where you may assume a distribution leadership position. For instance, smaller companies are not great targets for large accounting firms because of cost structure and overhead. The billing rate for large firms is typically more expensive due to factors like the number of people required to serve large clients, the overhead of maintaining offices and large IT systems to manage the practice, the breadth of services that a large firm needs to offer, and the complexity of those services. It usually isn't cost-effective for the big firm to take on small clients.

This provides an opportunity to serve smaller companies or partner with a large firm to reach those smaller clients. Getting referrals from larger firms and establishing a strong relationship would be one way to establish a distribution leadership position. It would be difficult for a competitor to challenge you if the larger firm is recommending you as its preferred partner.

Can you own the distribution position to reach your target customers and serve them better than a bigger firm due to fewer cost and price pressures? If so, that may be a segment you want to pursue.

But you also need to understand barriers keeping other businesses out of those spaces. It may be that the distribution channel doesn't make sense for you or them because there are some inherent problems with the channel. For example, maybe the larger accounting firms won't recommend anyone to smaller potential clients because of liability issues. It may be possible to find creative ways to work with the larger firm to get access to those potential clients without directly using them as a reference. Perhaps you can purchase leads from them.

These are the types of things you are hoping to uncover when doing a competitive analysis. What messaging or claims do your competitors make? Do they resonate with your target customers? Does their messaging contain items that customers care about that you could be missing? Your review of the completed feature analysis should leave you with clear areas of differentiation between you and your competitors. That enables you to exploit those areas with your messaging and product offerings.

Profitability Impact Analysis—Porter's Five Forces

In Chapter 2, we discussed Porter's Five Forces, the five competitive analysis areas that help illuminate the impact on profitability due to competitive or supplier advantages.

The five forces entail understanding:

- The impact of direct competitors in the industry
- The potential of new entrants coming into the sector
- The power of the suppliers over you
- The power of the customers over you
- The threats of substitutes

In this chapter, we will ignore the power of suppliers and customers. Instead, we'll focus on the industry competition, the potential of new industry entrants, and the threat of substitute products. Let's use our ice cream sandwich retail outlet as an example.

In this case, one competitor to our business would be other ice cream sandwich specialty shops. We learn that two such shops exist in our location that offer direct, competitive products. Both have similar offerings and apply comparable messaging and advertising.

The significant differentiators among the two other ice cream sandwich competitors and our company are the pricing, the number of cookies that could be selected for the sandwiches, and the variety of ice cream flavors.

However, we may discover that the most crucial differentiators are variations in price and the number of flavors. Understanding the feature and price differences between our offerings and the competitors' offerings gives us knowledge of how we stack up against the two other players in the eyes of the target customer.

But that's only one type of competition. Another would be a potential new entry into the market.

Many ice cream stores exist throughout the country. Any one of them could easily add cookies and toppings to their offerings and become new industry entrants. If Massachusetts-headquartered Baskin-Robbins, which has more than 5,000 outlets around the country, decided that it wanted to get into this space and offer cookies to build sandwiches, the company would be a formidable competitor. In fact, Baskin-Robbins began doing this very thing in 2016. It would be unlikely that it would offer the same number of cookie flavors and ice cream flavors that our company does because cookies are not its primary business. This potential variation would be something to understand because it would become a messaging and competitive differentiator between Baskin-Robbins and our ice cream sandwich shop. A new entrant could immediately affect the pricing and demand for our business's products, so monitoring this would be an important ongoing task.

The third area is the threat of substitute products. Substitute products are things that can be used by customers to fulfill a need without being a direct competitor. While they don't directly compete with our product or service, they may be chosen by a potential customer instead of our product or service because they are close enough to what we offer.

Ice cream sandwiches sold in grocery stores represent a substitute product for the cookie ice cream sandwich we make in our store. To analyze this threat, we would make a table similar to the one we created to assess the features of our direct competitors. In this new table, we would look at the different types of ice cream cookie or ice cream sandwich products in the freezer section of the grocery store and try to understand the features and messaging differences from our ice cream sandwich store.

Evaluating each of these three different areas contributes to a robust competitive analysis.

Of the wide range of approaches and templates for doing competitive analyses, there are two that are useful for the strategic plan stage. The first of these approaches is the competitive analysis chart, enabling a comparison of your business to direct competitors, as we outlined through the grocery store competitive analysis in Chapter 3.

The columns in the competitive analysis chart are up to you, but the best way to do this is to think through the 5 to 10 leading decision factors that customers face when buying your product or selecting your service. In almost all cases, price will be one of the leading factors. Make sure to include this in your assessment. Let's conduct a competitive analysis of the ice cream sandwich business.

	Our Ice Cream Dessert Shop	Chain Competitor #1	Competitor #2	Competitor #3
Type of Store	In-store dining and walk-up window	In-store dining	In-store dining and walk-up window	Walk-up window only
Size of Store/Tables	Medium— seating for 25	Medium— seating for 30	Small—three tables (12 max)	N/A— walk-up only
Ice Cream Flavors	30—rotate weekly	Up to 32	10	10
Cookie Flavors	5 cookie types	5 cookie types	Ice cream only	Ice cream only
Other Baked Items	Brownies	Cake, pies	No	No
Vegan Options	Yes, vegan ice-cream options	No	Yes, vegan ice-cream options	No
Gluten-Free Options	Yes	No	No	No

	Our Ice Cream Dessert Shop	Chain Competitor #1	Competitor #2	Competitor #3
Nondairy Options	Yes, but contains egg	No	No	No
Catering Option	Yes, and delivery	Yes	Yes, and delivery	No
Unique Offerings	Ice cream and cookies, brownie sundaes, wide range of dietary options	Overall dessert offerings, (ice cream, cookies, cakes, pies)	Convenience	Convenience

Figure 7.2 Ice cream sandwich business competitive analysis chart

In the analysis chart, you will see that we identified both cookie offerings and ice cream flavor offerings as decision points. We also added vegan and gluten-free options as decision points. Those tend to be things that people look at when deciding where to go. Any advantages you have in these areas should be highlighted in your messaging to customers. Suppose every one of the competitors has these options. In that case, there isn't a competitive advantage. Still, *not* messaging that you also have these options could be a competitive disadvantage: Potential customers may be going to your competitors because they don't realize that you also have vegan or gluten-free options.

Another approach is a strengths, weaknesses, opportunities, and threats (SWOT) analysis. A SWOT analysis is a framework used to evaluate a business's or a product's competitive position to understand where there are opportunities to communicate strengths and where there is a need to address weaknesses. A SWOT analysis assesses the internal forces by examining the strengths and weaknesses that we can control. It also allows for the exploration of external factors, out of your control, that are opportunities to exploit or threats for which we may prepare.

Try to understand from a customer's perspective how they view your offering and your direct competitors' offerings and why they should choose you and your product over the competition. Look for opportunities to differentiate your offerings across the product, pricing, distribution, and messaging spectrum. Building a comprehensive competitive analysis in those areas will provide insight into what is

STRENGTHS

- High quality ice cream
- Fresh baked cookies
- Many topping options
- Prime locations
- Strong local brand

WEAKNESSES

- Limited options for dairy-free, vegan, or gluten-free
- Hard to forecast cookie production accurately due to many options
- Cost of raw materials due to premium focus

OPPORTUNITIES

- Simplifying list of cookie options
- Offering natural and diet-friendly options
- Broadening the type of dessert products offered (shakes, sundaes, etc)

THREATS

- National brand ice cream retailer within one mile of us
- Increasing costs due to pandemic or supply chain issues
- Ice cream sandwiches no longer desired as a dessert

OPPORTUNITIES TO OPTIMIZE

RISKS TO BUSINESS

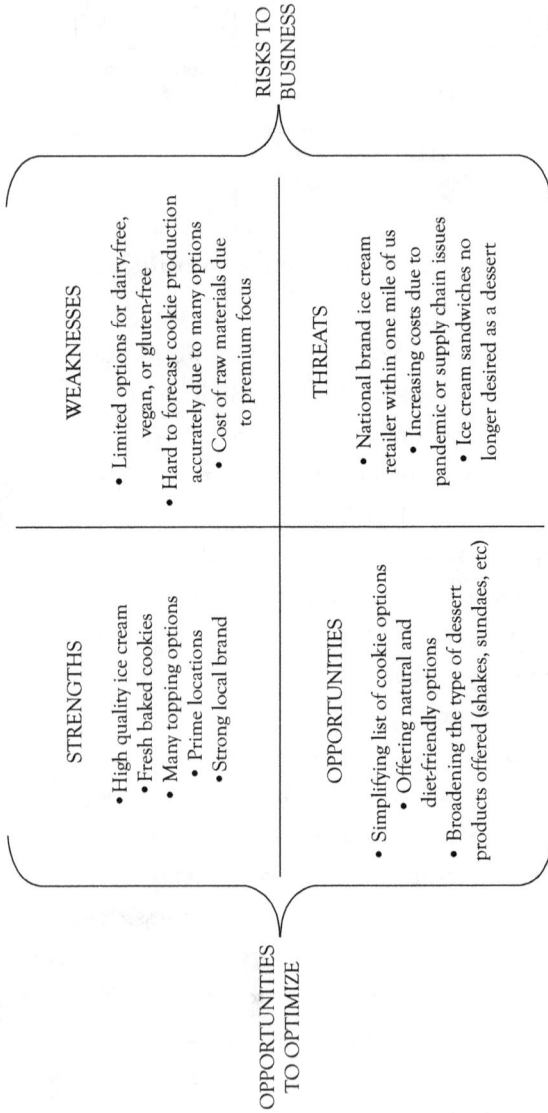

Figure 7.3 SWOT analysis chart for the ice cream sandwich shop

required to have a supremely competitive product or service offering. Later, we will go deeper into how the competitive analysis findings will help your business.

Key takeaways from this chapter:

1. Gaining insight into your competitors' strengths and weaknesses is essential for formulating an effective marketing strategy.
2. A comprehensive competitive analysis evaluates aspects such as competitors' products, target customer segments, messaging, pricing, and sales strategies.
3. A business competitive analysis investigates and contrasts competitors' approaches to addressing the top 5 to 10 factors that influence customer decisions when choosing a company for purchasing products or services similar to your offerings.
4. A product or service feature analysis scrutinizes the distinctions in features, pricing, and support between your offerings and those of your competitors.

CHAPTER 8

Delivering Winning Products and Services

As we have discussed throughout this book, business is about exchanging value between your company and the customer. Much of marketing consists of managing the exchange of value: the customer obtains a product or service that delights them, and the organization obtains profit and goodwill.

In a large company with a sizeable marketing department, this managing of the elements of value is often handled by different marketing teams. Corporate marketing generally manages the communications and marketing around the company brand. Product teams generally manage the marketing functions around specific products or services. Even within product teams, product marketing and product management are often two different jobs. Product marketing usually focuses on developing marketing communications and advertising around products. Product management deals with core product development and execution issues such as:

- Understanding who the customer is and what the customer wants
- Understanding what products and features are needed for those customers
- Determining how you'll position the products with respect to the competition
- Developing the key messages that highlight the product or service value based on product understanding and its features for the specific customers
- Setting the price range that is acceptable to customers while also ensuring that you maximize your gross profit (price minus cost)

In many small- and mid-sized businesses, product marketing and product management are combined. The person who determines who the target customers are is also involved in determining the right product or service features for the products being offered, the key messages that will be advertised to customers, and the pricing for the product. In many cases, it's the person who owns or runs the business. In this chapter, we'll focus on product management and product marketing together as a function rather than as a job.

It's difficult, if not impossible, to deliver a product or service that delights the customer if you don't have a clear idea of what the customer is looking for. This customer response will be different depending on the circumstances. Offering a product or service known to the customer or market, such as tax service, will elicit a different response than something unique to the market, such as a new menu item or bike model.

If a product is known to the market, characteristics including features, price, purchase process, and convenience may be the key things that drive a customer to buy your product or service. In that case, understanding how your product lines up versus competitor options will help identify where you have opportunities to shine and where you have risks or challenges to closing a sale.

As you think about what is important to customers when they make purchase decisions, two main elements should come to mind. One is the specific features presented about the product or service. For example, a road bike consists of product features such as a frame, gears, rims, and handlebars. Customers may desire a carbon fiber frame over an aluminum frame. If so, that would be valuable for you to communicate.

The second element is the product's or service's benefits. Continuing the example of the road bike, custom fitting the bike to an individual would be a benefit that provides a competitive advantage if other bike sellers don't offer that service. Or a better warranty could sway a purchase decision your way.

It is critical to understand the features and benefits that your products offer compared to the competition. Prospective customers do this with almost every purchase. Think about a product you purchased during your last grocery shopping experience. You likely compared the product to other similar products on the shelf. What was your thought process at the time? You may have considered the size of the package (feature). You may have thought about how the packaging affected the product's shelf life (benefit). You likely thought about price. This is how almost all purchase decisions are made. People spend as much time and energy evaluating features and benefits as the price for the product or service increases. Considering different egg purchase options in the grocery store takes seconds. Considering a new insurance product or a car purchase can often take hours, days, or weeks.

If your product is known to the market, you should consider the products that are in direct competition with it. Then compare the features that are the key decision factors for customers buying the product. Experience has taught us that the 80/20 rule works here. That is, 80 percent of the purchase decision is usually defined by a small number of factors. The 80/20 approach states that 80 percent of results come from only 20 percent of all of the possible reasons that exist for some event or activity (like a purchase). In marketing, the goal is to use the rule to identify the top decision points (the 20 percent) that drive why most customers make a purchase in the category in which you compete. Identifying those decision points allows you to focus your marketing efforts on the criteria that 80 percent of which purchases are made. A good general rule: 10 to 15 comparison variables are usually more than enough to assess the important decision points that a potential customer will likely make for a product or service. You don't need to match the features 100 percent. The remaining reasons why buyers would select a product or service likely have little appeal to most prospective customers.

Existing Product or a New Product?

You should also consider whether you are marketing a product or service in a market area that potential customers already know or whether you are introducing something new that they don't yet know they need or want. If it's introducing a product or service into an existing market space, then you must be aware of competitors. If it's a completely new market or product space, then you need to think about potential alternative products to what you are offering—and who the potential new competitors could be.

In the fast-food industry, for example, customers already know McDonald's and Burger King. Those customers are deciding between Big Macs, Quarter Pounders, or Double Cheeseburgers from McDonald's, or a Whopper with Cheese or a Double Cheeseburger from Burger King.

Each company typically communicates product traits, including the size and number of beef patties, bun type, and price, to attract customers.

The McRib sandwich, on the other hand, is a different product offering. Potential customers might not have a clue about what this is or why they should buy it. The role of marketing, in this case, is to work with product development to understand the features of the product that appeals to customers. Then the marketing team communicates those features to the broader public.

If your product or service is one the public knows, then focus on features that also are known and expected by those customers. Those features are what determine a customer's decision to buy one product over another. In a bike purchase, the feature may be the materials used in the bike frame. Or it may be a bike's total number of gears. Ignoring the gearing or frame materials would be foolish. Those may represent important decision points for prospective customers.

In the case of a new product offering, you need to concentrate on the new features but also highlight the utility of known features and services.

Let's go back to our tax preparer example. Investment planning could be a new service offering. To optimize adoption by potential customers, we would connect the new investment planning service to the tax preparation work already being done. We might say to potential customers, "I'm a tax planner, and I can help you with your investment decisions based on your tax situation because I also can work on your taxes."

By doing so, we're emphasizing the new product or feature in addition to the feature that people already know.

Prospective customers likely would respond positively: "My current tax accountant doesn't help me with investments. I can get two services with one service provider, and maybe that's a better solution."

Using the ice cream sandwich shop example, we might offer a well-known brand of ice cream in our sandwich. That would differentiate our product, despite our store offering the same kind of sandwich as our competitors.

An ice cream sandwich is a well-known product to customers. So, focusing on the well-known brand of ice cream in that sandwich may give a competitive edge.

The four major product management elements that you need to think about in the marketing process are:

- The features that the product or services provide
- Price
- The benefits that a customer gets
- How the offering is superior to the competition

Often overlooked, talking to customers directly is a crucial aspect of product marketing. It helps you gain an understanding of other features and benefits that may be important to their purchase decision but were not obvious to you before. Those conversations frequently lead to "aha" moments that you can test with other customers to find new areas of strength or opportunity against your competition.

When conducting market research, a good, practical way to do this is to create two lists of your product or service's desired features or benefits that are important to prospective customers.

The first list would identify the perceived barriers that might prevent a potential customer from buying your product or service. These barriers could be related to the product or your competition. Think again from the features or benefits perspective. In the bike example, it could be that customers don't buy our bikes because they are too heavy, or they don't look sleek, or the price seems too high compared to the competition. These are things that we can work with. Can we get data to show that they aren't too heavy? Can we do a better job explaining why our bikes are more expensive? Are the materials that we use better than the competitions? Would that justify the price? This list provides clarity about the things that prospective customers may be thinking when considering purchasing one of our bikes. Understanding these potential barriers is a critical component of your marketing strategy journey. Some of this feedback may need to go back to the developers or the purchasing people in your company, so they may reduce the price of your product without reducing your profitability. Some of the feedback may drive improvements or changes to your offering.

Your customer research should result in knowledge of the top characteristics customers are looking for in the product or service as well as a good idea of what's not optimal in the products currently on the market.

The goal is to learn what is on the customers' wish lists. So, pay attention when they say things like, "I wish products would do [insert the desired outcome] better." Or "I wish products had [this feature]."

The second list, your "dream list," should be based on the following question: "In a perfect world with no limitations, what would the product or service offer you that you cannot get today?" This dream list provides you with insight into development opportunities that, if you can deliver, would result in an advantage over your competition.

If done with the intent of understanding what is important to your target customer, these two lists will allow you to focus on the features that drive buying behavior. It also will reveal features or services that may be valuable to develop in the future to maintain a competitive edge in the marketplace.

In your research with customers, you will likely get responses that seem unrealistic or outside of the scope of the product or service sold today. Don't ignore these. Add them to your dream list. While they might not be applicable to today's offerings, these responses may be appropriate to consider for future offerings or for future development, especially if many provide similar feedback. If they are telling you about these wants or needs, they are probably also telling your competitors. If a competitor were eventually able to offer any of these features, what would that do to your ability to attract customers?

The first list enables you to learn what customers consider valuable today. If you can solve any of the things on that list with your current products or services, this is where you should consider crafting your marketing messages regarding what you currently have available in the market. The second list provides insight into what your future products or services will need if you want to remain competitive in the marketplace.

Your marketing strategy should address the important frustration points raised by your potential customers. To exploit any advantage, you'd communicate things that you currently are able to do from the lists through advertising and marketing communications such as social media, news media, conference or community event participation, and other communications channels.

Creating the wish list often yields a surprise: your product may already offer precisely what potential customers say they want or wish for, but you haven't communicated it effectively. This exercise helps to improve your product messaging.

It's possible to learn that product features or service offerings on your internal development list turn out to be things customers don't care about. In that way, this exercise also hones your focus on what matters to customers and where you need to invest your development efforts.

It is crucial to talk to people who don't yet know about your product or service. It is a mistake to speak only to existing customers or to people who aren't yet customers due to different expectations and needs.

Another source of insight is past customers you have lost to competitors or who haven't bought your product in some time. In the example of the bike store, what if it reached out to one of its former bike customers? Have they made another bike purchase since they bought it from the bike shop? If so, why did they choose not to purchase from the bike shop again? Those insights are critical in understanding what is driving customer purchase decisions.

When doing customer research such as this, talking to one or two people is not enough. It is imperative that you speak with enough people within your desired customer segments to see clear patterns that emerge. There isn't a specific number. The sample size depends on the type of product and service. Large organizations have access to market research resources and agencies that have formulas and repeatable processes for doing this type of research.

We've used the term "characterizing" to describe the competition and the prospective customer segments. This market research also helps to characterize the product or service-offering segments.

Even in larger organizations, many senior executives engage in listening to and evaluating some of the market research interviews because they can pick up on nuances that don't come out in a report. Product or service enhancement is vital to maintaining a competitive position. Competitors don't stand still.

Larger companies frequently employ teams focused on keeping products updated and fresh. In many large marketing organizations, this function is called "sustaining product marketing."

Your competitive analysis and customer desire lists enable you to see where your offerings provide value to customers relative to your competition. These exercises also help you understand the opportunities that exist to improve your product offerings and messaging. Doing so enhances product appeal and attracts customers.

Prioritizing Customer Market Research Feedback

An additional step you can take to optimize your understanding of the space is to identify customers' prioritization of existing or future product features. While you now should have a list of the needs from the market research you conducted you may find that it is too much information to make decisions from. You will need to prioritize these desired or expected needs and wants in a way that is actionable and also has relevance to your marketing efforts.

A first step in making sense of the information is identifying the high-priority elements that customers shared. High-priority features or elements are considered "table stakes" as they are the important competitive decision features. Examples of these elements for evaluating a fast-food burger chain's various burger offerings include price, number of hamburger patties, and with or without cheese.

These are the high-level things that customers will consider. If they are not in a customer's zone of expectation, then that customer will move on.

In our fast-food example, second-tier traits include the type of bun, such as sesame, brioche, or pretzel.

If in the futures or "dream" list, there existed a number of customers who said things like, "I wish that there were different types of cheeses," or "I'd love hamburgers on a Hawaiian sweet bread roll," you might consider offering them to enhance your product and attract new customers.

Characterizing the needs and wants of customers around products and services is necessary. Managing the products that you offer and develop for your customers requires you to do so. Providing insights that help you identify the important messages to prospective customers is another benefit.

This work of evaluating where your product stands compared to the competition and what your customers value allows you to focus on optimizing your offering in a way that provides you with a competitive advantage.

The exercises also provide a roadmap for future product development. One mistake companies sometimes make is adding features to products and services that aren't valued by customers yet but cost the company money to include with the product.

Think about the last cell phone you purchased. Many phones have applications that may seem unnecessary to you. They had no value in your purchase decision. From the phone manufacturer's perspective, however, those applications usually have a licensing fee. If the phone manufacturer has to pay the licensing fee to include the application, then that is product-cost money spent that isn't being valued by the customer. That results in lost profit. They could have sold the phone for the same price without the software and license costs. But you also may notice that many of those apps require a customer to sign up and pay a separate fee. In that case, the application vendor may be paying the phone manufacturer to include the app so that new customers will use it.

A more formal way to further this research is through a process called conjoint analysis. This is frequently done in larger organizations with the resources, time, and budgets to do these more complex analyses. Conjoint analysis is a process that uses statistical methods to help understand how important a feature is and how people value the product's features and benefits. It's an important tool to use when making expensive development investments in a product. It is not used as often in easily modified products or services. We won't be digging any deeper into the process of conjoint analysis in this book because there is enough information and insight that a marketer can gather by starting with the approach that we discussed here. Just know that it is commonly used in larger companies, and you may be interested in exploring it further as you get more comfortable with collecting market research data.

The next step in building our strategy is to take the information you've discovered and place it into the Strategic Marketing Framework. You will probably have a pretty good feel, based on your first top-10 list of customer priorities, what features will be important to the product user and product customer or buyer.

Remember, those two groups may be the same, but often they are not. It's important to think about the product priorities from the perspective of the user and the buyer.

Here is an example of how you would map out the Strategic Marketing Framework for our bike shop.

SEGMENT/ PRODUCT LINE Specify targets	LINE 1 Mountain Bikes		LINE 2 Road Bikes		
PEOPLE Identify and describe those you're targeting	USER Bike rider	CUSTOMER Bike rider or parent for younger bikers	USER Bike rider	CUSTOMER Bike rider or parent of younger bikers	
PRODUCT/ FEATURES Identify key products or features for users and customers	Frame type Bike size Aesthetics Component makers	Price Warranty User reviews Personalized bike fitting	Frame material and stiffness Bike size Weight Gear type	Price Warranty Breadth of options Service capability	U P S T R E A M
STRATEGIC MARKETING GOALS What are you trying to achieve?					
COMPETITION Who are you up against?	Online (Amazon, eBay) Bikes R Us (within 20 mi) REI Academy Outdoors		Online (Amazon, eBay) Bikes R Us (within 20 mi) Walmart, Target, Academy Outdoors		

Figure 8.1 Bike Business Features Example

Examining the framework, you should see some things beginning to tie together.

Riders, or users, of mountain bikes, for instance, likely care about the type and size of the frames and the makers of key components such as gear shifts, front forks, and wheel rims.

The bike buyer, even if the buyer and rider are one and the same, likely puts a priority on price, warranty, and user reviews. Both the buyer and the rider may care about getting the bike personally fit.

In the competition section, you may also begin to piece together where the bike company can differentiate its offerings from those of the competition. Perhaps its bikes can't be as inexpensive as online competitors. But what about offering personalized bike fittings? That could be a competitive advantage point to push in the marketing messages.

An overarching goal is to continuously try to figure out what features customers are willing to pay for and what features they aren't. This reveals the changes that are necessary for your product or service to be a market leader.

At this point, you have identified the customer segments, done your competitive analysis, and spoken to current and prospective customers from those segments. You have a clear list of things they value, things that need to be changed, and in a perfect world, the features or services you should provide for them.

Now you can better understand your product or service offerings relative to the competition. Because you have done this work, you also have an idea about what moves you can make regarding your product pricing.

In the following chapters, we'll talk about how this information affects pricing.

Key takeaways from this chapter:

1. In large organizations, marketing activities are often distributed across various departments, such as corporate marketing, product marketing, product management, and marketing communications. However, these functions are typically combined within a single marketing team in startups and small businesses.

2. Marketing challenges and strategies differ between products or services that potential customers are already familiar with and those that are entirely new. Entirely new products or services require introducing the features and benefits and clarifying their applications and value.

3. Four primary product management aspects to consider are the features provided by the product or service, the benefits to customers, pricing, and competitive positioning relative to rival offerings.

4. Conducting customer research reveals potential customers' priorities regarding product or service features and requirements.

CHAPTER 9

Developing the Key Messages

Communicating information about your products or services and the reasons why customers should buy from you is one of the most important roles of marketing. This can be done through traditional advertising on TV or radio or in newspapers, magazines, and other publications. It may be done through social media marketing on platforms such as Facebook, Instagram, and TikTok.

Search engine optimization (SEO) marketing is another option. The term means ensuring that your web pages and social media content include keywords people use when searching for products or services like yours. Optimizing your web content for search engines can impact the location of your company or products in the order that they appear in search results. SEO marketing can also refer to paying for higher placement in the search results through a method called paid search.

Communicating to potential users about your product or service may also be done by engaging journalists and industry-specific analysts by encouraging them to write about your product. News stories, product reviews, or press releases about your company are ways to get the message out about your business.

What matters is that messaging through these channels yields a desired action or behavior from prospective customers.

A common error that marketers make is focusing on developing, producing, and executing advertising and social-media communications that lack coherence or fail to deliver results.

Developing messages that effectively highlight business and product offerings that spur positive responses from potential customers can potentially create more value than an ad or content placement. Facebook display ads and high-ranking Google search results are worthwhile only if they deliver the desired actions. Those include visits to your website, customers contacting your company, or a product purchase. Otherwise, you're wasting time, energy, and dollars.

Effective messaging requires determining your goal and with whom you're trying to achieve it, then conveying messaging that delivers that aim. This represents the starting point of communicating your value proposition. The work you've done to identify customer segments helps. Remember: users and customers may vary. Craft messaging appropriate to the relevant audience, catering to their respective desires.

Effective messaging communicates why a customer should take a particular action. For example, effective messaging by a restaurant could communicate the style and quality of its food while also offering a compelling reason why a customer would want to eat that food or visit the restaurant.

Some messaging campaigns exist only to drive brand awareness. Large companies with deep resources, however, are more likely to take that approach than small businesses with smaller budgets. Brand messaging is a good approach for helping drive awareness, but it can be costly and take time to develop the desired results.

Marketing communications by small- and mid-sized companies generally should focus on driving the desired behavior of targeted customer prospects. Good advertising does this well. Great advertising does this while also building brand awareness.

A message map is among the methods some marketers use to create powerful messages in advertising and other types of marketing communication. A message map elucidates what messages you want to convey to prospective customers, advertising partners, and marketing partners.

A message map typically contains more than 4 but fewer than 10 key messages that you want to continually communicate about your offerings.

Those messages should be informed by what we've already learned regarding your product or service features that your user and customer segments consider important.

The message map always begins with the company's value proposition. It answers the questions:

- Why should people do business with you?
- What is unique about your company, products, or services?

A value proposition that might exist at our bike shop could be: "We provide riders with the most up-to-date bike technology with the most comfortable fit at the most competitive price in the market." We'd place that value proposition at the top of our message map. In total, 4 to 10 key message points would support that value proposition.

The value proposition is what you want your customers, prospective customers, suppliers, and partners to think about you when they consider your business. Your main value proposition should be something that is actually valuable to customers.

You should begin to select and build your strategic messages by reexamining your competitor analysis. Use the differentiators your think are beneficial to your customers and users and highlight those. Remember: your marketing communications should reflect how your company is distinct from your competitors and why customers should buy from you.

Among our bike shop's differentiators are experts who provide riders with custom bike fittings. The strategic message on the message map may be that we provide the best fit for customers. Or it could be that we sell bikes that are comfortable for riders. We then supply proof points supporting the promise. One proof point could be that we have custom fitters that will provide the service in the store. Another proof point could be that we have special bike components that make riding more comfortable, which customer ratings explicitly state.

The messaging map should have talking points that support your claims. You should be able to defend any competitive advantage you claim by providing enough proof points to leave no doubt in your customers' minds that you are the right choice for their purchase decision even if competitors make the identical claim.

Fast-food restaurants, for example, often sell double cheeseburgers. Each chain claims that its burgers are the best. But undergirding that value proposition are key messaging points. That language includes the perks that come with the burgers at McDonald's or Burger King: superior pickles, special sauce, lettuce, and cheese.

There are several ways to express the core value proposition and key messages while we build the message map:

- Price positioning versus the competition
- Company, product, or service capabilities

- Customer service and support options
- Implementation assistance the company provides upon acquiring and using the product or service
- Establishment and cultivation of the customer-company relationship

Message delivery, specifically through appropriate channels, is essential. Options include advertising, sales promotions, personal selling, public relations, and direct marketing. The method chosen depends on the goal. The delivery mechanism varies according to the channel. We'll discuss channel differences in greater detail in a later chapter.

Channel examples include personal selling, where a salesperson or customer-facing staff member speaks directly with customers. Another is distributing a press release to journalists or conducting interviews with reporters and analysts to yield press coverage. Direct marketing, on the other hand, entails sending mailers to homes or e-mails directly to prospects.

Figure 9.1 Key messaging channels

A communication strategy that is poorly thought out may result in inconsistent messaging. Deploying all these channels simultaneously to reach customers without coordination of messaging can negatively impact your marketing. Such an approach—which, unfortunately, does happen—accomplishes nothing except to confuse prospective customers.

Companies seek to communicate with customers for an array of reasons:

- To inform about offerings
- To raise awareness of what your company does, who you are, and what you provide
- To persuade them to take a specific action such as visit your store or website, buy a product, or sign a contract
- To contrast your company with the competition

Computer manufacturers, for example, commonly compare their features and benefits to competitors' offerings regarding notebooks, desktop computers, and phones.

Apple and Samsung frequently show what differentiates their products from the competition. The latter's 2021 commercials for the Samsung S21 Ultra highlighted what they deemed "epic video," which highlighted filming in 8K. Samsung describes this type of video as cinema-quality while also being able to maintain long battery life and get still photos from the video stream. Apple ran video advertising in the same period for its iPhone 13 with the tagline "Work All Day," which highlighted ruggedness and reliability with moisture resistance and a ceramic shield on the phone surface. The ad also stressed high-speed processing and 5G wireless connections. While Apple briefly mentions cinema mode, the main message is about a device designed to help users integrate the phone into their daily work lives.

It's rare for a company to call out a competitor directly, and for good reason. If you make a claim about a competitor's product that is not correct, it could result in a lawsuit. Still, it's crucial to send messages that enable customers to identify what differentiates the offering from the competitors. The message that reaches the prospective customer should be: "We are the best choice for you."

Reminding customers about the value proposition is among the most fundamental goals of advertising and messaging. In today's nonstop media-rich world, cutting through the noise with such messaging is strategically significant.

Messaging also keeps customers engaged with a company. A single-item purchase or service contract is much less valuable than a long-term relationship. The latter results in greater revenue generation over a period of time. The metric used to capture the value of such a long-term relationship is what we introduced in an earlier chapter as "customer lifetime value" (CLV). That value increases if your company ensures the customer remembers what you have to offer and continues to purchase from you.

Let's use our tax preparation example to illustrate this within the strategic framework. H&R Block is particularly effective in this area of its messaging. It advertises to new customers while also reminding past customers to return. The company communicates that it has the taxpayer's information and reminds all taxpayers annually when tax season arrives. In this way, H&R Block establishes itself in customers' minds as their preferred partner due to a continuing, mutually beneficial relationship. This type of messaging effectively deters competitors from poaching existing customers. Additionally, H&R Block also offers small business bookkeeping services at what it describes as significantly below standard accountants' rates. H&R Block can identify messages that resonate with potential clients for either tax services or bookkeeping services.

Now let's build the message map. How do you do this? Start with the main positioning statement or a value statement. What is the main thing you want customers to remember? Next, you identify and select the key messages that differentiate your product or service from that of your competitors. These key messages are your anchoring messages—the things you intend to have your target customers know and remember about you.

It doesn't make much sense to select a key message that is the same as everyone else's. "We do taxes" is not a key message. Every accounting firm says that. What is the key message? It could be that we have the best accountants or bookkeepers and/or that we're known for the lowest audit rates in the industry. Those would be key messages because they are differentiators. They communicate *our* message. They differentiate us from other tax service providers.

Next, start building the proof points under each key anchor message. Your proof point messages not only support the key anchor point, but they are also opportunities to include content creation, advertising, and even promotions. The message map helps focus your execution in the market so that, over time, you build brand awareness and a brand position that is defensible against the competition.

After you build the message map, it becomes necessary to test it. What you believe are the key messages might not resonate with your target customers. The customers decide what they want to respond to, not you. Test your hypothesis key messages with existing customers and potential customers. Find out which messages resonate and which don't.

There are a number of ways to test your key messages. Some are qualitative. Some are quantitative. One quantitative way is to use a method called A/B testing, where you make two different versions of the same advertisement or social media post with different key messages and use the site analytics (such as the Facebook Ad results or Google Analytics) to see which generates a better response. A qualitative approach to testing your key messages is to present them to prospective customers and existing customers for your product or service and ask the following questions:

- Is this message clear and concise?
- Does the message resonate with you? (Does it "hook" the person into learning more?)
- Does the message seem factual? Is it believable?
- Is the message compelling and worth pursuing?
- Does it seem different, or better, than what other companies offer?
- Do you understand the value of what we are messaging?

There are many ways to test key messages and many tools and paid services that can help improve them. A simple Google search on "testing key messages" will result in a massive list of articles and services to help

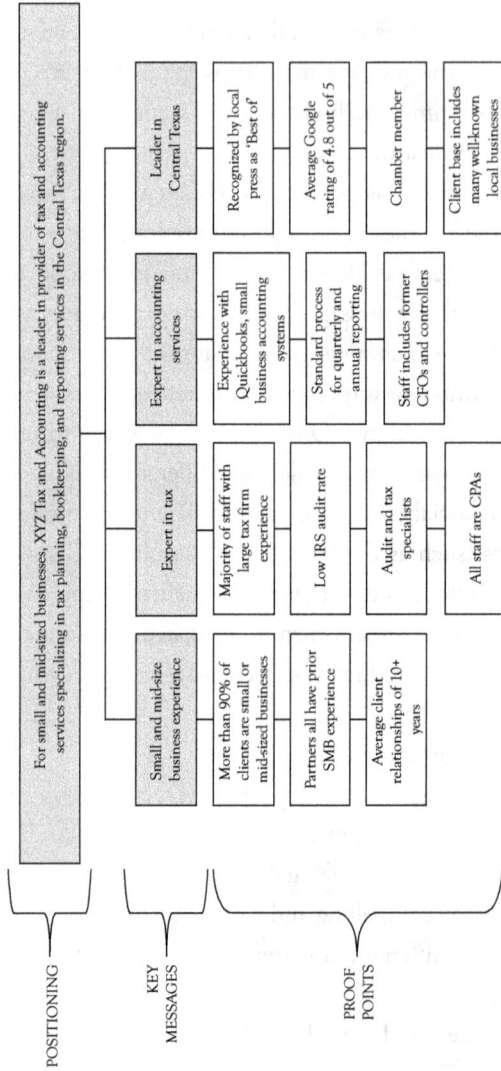

POSITIONING	For small and mid-sized businesses, XYZ Tax and Accounting is a leader in provider of tax and accounting services specializing in tax planning, bookkeeping, and reporting services in the Central Texas region.			
KEY MESSAGES	Small and mid-size business experience	Expert in tax	Expert in accounting services	Leader in Central Texas
PROOF POINTS	More than 90% of clients are small or mid-sized businesses	Majority of staff with large tax firm experience	Experience with Quickbooks, small business accounting systems	Recognized by local press as 'Best of'
	Partners all have prior SMB experience	Low IRS audit rate	Standard process for quarterly and annual reporting	Average Google rating of 4.8 out of 5
	Average client relationships of 10+ years	Audit and tax specialists	Staff includes former CFOs and controllers	Chamber member
		All staff are CPAs		Client base includes many well-known local businesses

Figure 9.2 Key message map

you develop and test yours. Whatever path or approach you take, testing your key messages is important to ensure that they result in the intended response.

Review and test your message map on a regular basis to ensure communication continues to resonate with customers. Reviewing your messaging while also assessing your competition's advertising and messaging can yield business intelligence on how your competitors have responded to your messaging. Competitors will attempt to understand your company's value proposition and best it. Or they might attempt to undercut your company by demonstrating that your value proposition is worth less than what your company's messaging claims. Among the things to observe regarding your competitors:

- Are they responding to you?
- Are they trying to take away some of your key position points?
- Are they taking a different path that's resonating more with customers?

It's time to get back to your Strategic Marketing Framework. If you've done the exercise with prospective and current customers well and developed some key messages that resonate, you will want to incorporate them into your framework. Below is how this would look for our accounting firm:

SEGMENT/ PRODUCT LINE Specify targets	LINE 1 Business Customers (bookkeeping and tax)		LINE 2 Individual Tax Preparation	
PEOPLE Identify and describe those you're targeting	USER Executives Board Members Tax Authorities Lenders (banks)	CUS- TOMER Bus < 25 employees Finance or accounting manager	USER Individuals Spouse (filing jointly or family)	CUSTOMER Person responsible for tax filing

(Continues)

(*Continued*)

PRODUCT/ FEATURES Identify key products or features for users and customers	Reliable financial reports Tax filings on time Timely availability	Cost Guidance on tax planning Reliability No tax or report issues	Completeness of return Maximizing refunds/ limiting taxes due	Cost Timing/ Accuracy Maximizing refunds/limiting taxes due	U P S T R E A M
STRATEGIC MARKETING GOALS What are you trying to achieve?					
COMPETITION Who are you up against?	National accounting firms Other local firms Online accounting systems (DIY)		Retail tax preparers Other local tax preparers Online tax prep platforms Tax preparation software		
PRICE POSITION Ideal position vs. competition or price strategy					
KEY MESSAGES What matters to users/customers	Deep financial and accounting expertise Cost-effective Responsive and reliable Broad technical capabilities		Experienced tax preparers History of happy customers Quality work Fast service		

Figure 9.3 Accounting business key message example

In the next chapter, we'll discuss different ways to deploy your messaging. We'll also explain the different channels to reach customers.

Key takeaways from this chapter:

1. A primary function of marketing is to effectively communicate accurate information about your products or services.
2. Many techniques and platforms can be employed to disseminate marketing messages.
3. A message map serves as a guide, detailing the essential messages to be conveyed to potential customers through advertising materials and public communication.
4. Marketing messages should begin with the core value proposition of your offering, followed by the supporting key messages.
5. Regularly evaluating your key messaging with both existing and prospective customers is vital.

CHAPTER 10

Understanding Pricing

The pricing of your company's product or service will have a demonstrable impact on the value equation. Price influences the customer's perception of what value they're receiving. Pricing also affects what profit a business captures.

While entire books have been written on pricing strategies, we're going to concentrate on pricing basics to help your small- and mid-sized business. In this chapter, we'll demonstrate how to integrate pricing blueprints into your marketing strategy.

Here are three simple pricing truths:

- Pricing low may increase demand and the number of happy customers but can often result in lower profit.
- Pricing high can increase profit but lower demand and customer satisfaction.
- Both strategies could cause problems for your business.

When setting prices, it's important for the marketer to know a few terms that are common in business finance: gross profit and net income and markup percentage.

Gross profit is the amount of profit that a product or service makes after subtracting the price that a customer pays from the direct costs (materials, labor, and shipping) to produce the product or service. If a product is sold for $1.50, and the direct costs to produce and deliver the product are $1.00, then the gross profit is $0.50. The calculation for gross profit shows how much you make after paying the costs of producing or selling your product or service. That $0.50 doesn't count for all of the costs, however. Indirect costs, such as allocations for the facilities, insurance, and general marketing, also exist. Subtracting the indirect costs from the gross profit tells you the operating income that your business receives from selling the product at the price and costs that are set. Some other additional costs (interest expenses, taxes) are applied to understand the net income. For pricing purposes, most marketers focus only on gross margins.

The term "markup percentage" is the amount added to the costs that result in the final price. For example, our product in the example above costs $1.00. A 20 percent markup percentage would be 20 percent of the cost ($1.00) or a price of $1.20. Understanding gross profit and markup is critical. There are several free online calculators available to help you when setting pricing.

At a more granular level, a price that's too low might not generate enough profit to cover costs. On the other hand, a price too high will cause customers to flock to competitors. The goal is to set a price that will yield satisfied customers, cover costs, and produce a profit.

Price Setting Methods

Many ways exist to set product and service pricing. It is important to avoid a one-size-fits-all approach. Product and market conditions are two factors that contribute to different pricing methods. The overall goal always is to capture maximum profit or value. With that in mind, adopted pricing methods should always consider what customers are willing to pay.

"Cost-plus pricing" or "cost-based pricing" is a common pricing method. While there are slight differences that pricing experts would argue about, the terms are often used interchangeably. Using this approach, the marketer adds the desired markup to the cost to produce the final product or service. Cost-plus pricing is done by adding the desired markup percentage to the cost of producing or acquiring the product or service. This cost can consist of any expense directly tied to the product or service delivery. For example, a pen maker wants to make the price 30 percent on every pen that it produces. Let's say that the cost of materials, direct labor, and shipping is $3.00 per pen. If the company wants a 30 percent markup, then the price to the customer would be $3.00 × 1.30 percent or $3.90 per pen. This is a common strategy due to its simplicity and predictability. The price moves with the direct costs to produce the product or service. The downside to cost-based pricing is that it ignores the effect of competitors' pricing.

Companies frequently deploy this approach when no clear information about competitive pricing, supply, or demand impact is available.

Contractors often use cost-plus pricing when they control projects and labor costs. Those are known costs. But contractors won't know what types of material they will use, how much of that material they will use, or the cost of that material until the job is done.

Cost-plus pricing enables contractors to ensure they'll earn a known amount of profit on the project regardless of the changes to material or labor costs. Prior to the COVID-19 pandemic, customers often accepted this pricing approach without question. Due to major material price increases and delivery delays; however, customers now often ask contractors more questions before agreeing to the proposed project.

A "competitive-pricing strategy" is one in which a business sets a price based on that of the competition.

Using this method requires knowing what other businesses are charging for similar offerings. Once you've established that, you can set your prices to lure customers from the competition. Factors such as your business's perceived market position and brand value must be considered. Then you may set prices above, below, or equal to your competition.

Competitive pricing is common when you're attempting to position your business in the market and/or against a well-known brand.

Think about big-box retailers that sell products at a lower price than other retailers—designer jeans at discount prices, for example. Walmart has a price-match policy that ensures it can always deliver lower prices than the competition to a customer. If a lower price is found elsewhere, Walmart will match it. If a customer presents a product from a competitor with a lower price than Walmart's, Walmart will reduce the price of its product on the spot to match it.

When using competitive pricing, the challenge that must be kept in mind is the costs of your service or product. If you aren't careful, it's possible to set prices that increase customers but end up losing you money. This is why successful businesses manage the costs of providing a product or service as aggressively as they manage to acquire customers.

"Value-based pricing," also known as "demand pricing," takes into account what the customer believes the worth is of the product or service. This approach is common when a consumer emotional connection, product scarcity, or a companion product or service exists that drives demand.

Apple customers, for example, are famously loyal to that company's products. Designer jewelry and clothes, by definition, are more difficult to obtain than mass-produced items in those categories. Printers that require ink cartridges or auto repair shops that offer additional services each cause consumers to spend more to acquire the add-on products or services to keep the primary product running.

Correctly done, value-based pricing requires an understanding of the customer's perceived value for the product or service and their familiarity with the competitive environment. Competitors can undercut value-based pricing if a business falls short of customer expectations.

Macroeconomic conditions also may impact customer buying decisions. Months of rising inflation during 2022, for example, created higher prices for goods and services across the board. A natural consumer reaction to such external dynamics is to curtail spending, particularly on things that seem too expensive.

An advantage of value-based pricing is that it can yield a higher profit than other pricing strategies. However, managing it properly requires intense customer focus and constant monitoring of the competitive environment and environmental conditions.

"Penetration pricing" is a strategy often used to attract customers to a new product or service with a lower price during its initial offering. Penetration pricing almost always includes the overall purchase price increasing through the addition of add-on options or additional features. The lower price helps a new product or service establish a presence in the market, begin to build a customer base, and attract customers from competitors. Penetration pricing is an effective tool to drive demand.

A new real estate agent, for instance, could decide to decrease the commission rate by 1 percent. The lower rate establishes the new agent in the real estate market and positions him or her as a less expensive alternative to the competition.

A new bike could start at a low base price, but additional features may be added to increase the price and margin. A new model bike may be offered at a substantial price below competitive models, but the addition of improved components such as different tires, gear shifters, or seats could substantially increase the price. The business encourages customers to add on to the purchase and will eventually reach a final price to maximize profit.

"Price skimming" also is an oft-used approach. The practice sets a high price initially, then lowers it as costs decrease or competitive pressures increase. All consumers have experienced this phenomenon with tech products, including laptops, wide-screen TVs, and smartphones.

Initially, there's a scarcity of supply or competitors. If the supply of products is finite and scarce, then pricing to meet a margin target (the gross margin desired) or to drive demand is unnecessary. Customers, such as those who used to wait for each new iPhone iteration, will pay more for a new or hard-to-obtain product.

Price skimming allows the business to maximize profits when there are limited products or services available in the marketplace. There may be limitations on the firm to make additional products or services available to the customers. If you can't produce enough product to fulfill customer demand—say there is a limit to how many bikes can be produced or how many ice cream sandwiches can be made in a workday—then don't price to increase demand. You are just giving away profit. Skimming is also used when there is limited availability of raw goods. Although, for some industries, there are legal limitations to how price skimming is done. Setting prices abnormally high during periods of shortages is called "price gouging." During a major water outage, charging significantly higher rates for bottled water would be considered price gouging and could be illegal. Federal law does not prohibit price gouging, and the practice is legal in many states. Simultaneously, however, a majority of states deter such profiteering.

Understanding Price and Demand Elasticity

Now that you understand some of the different approaches to pricing, it's essential to understand the concept of price-on-demand elasticity and inelasticity.

The concepts are straightforward. If demand has significant changes due to price, it is considered "elastic." If a price does not significantly affect demand, it's considered "inelastic." Take gas prices at the pump.

If the price moves a few cents, it doesn't dramatically affect demand. People still need gas. They will pay whatever price necessary to be able to drive their cars. Demand for gas is generally considered inelastic.

Products or services that see more pronounced changes in demand based on price are considered elastic. Products or services likely to see demand change, whether up or down, are those with many customer options or alternatives.

Restaurant food, for instance, is highly elastic because demand and choice fluctuate based on price.

Industries in which alternative solutions are available to customers experience fluctuating demand. Alternatives create an array of prices in the market, which, in turn, affect consumer demand for those options.

Tax preparation businesses discovered this the hard way when tax software and online services became common with the introduction of services such as Intuit's TurboTax, Quicken, and QuickBooks Online beginning in the 1980s. Pricing in this sector has experienced tremendous pressure for traditional tax preparation services because customers now may choose from many alternatives. When there are several options for customers to choose from, then demand for your product or service is going to change based on the pricing. Ensuring that a product or service is differentiated from the competition and offers unique value is essential to properly pricing and ensuring profitability.

The more differentiated a product or service is, or if it's unique, the less price generally affects demand. Clear differentiation is a good principle to understand and consider when pricing.

Bundling and Discounting

Driving and measuring revenue growth is crucial for growing a business. Two primary ways exist to drive revenue. One is to increase the number of customers that purchase a product or service at the average price. The other is to increase the total amount of the sale of the product or service by adding other products or services the customer will purchase.

This is where bundling comes in. Bundling is packaging multiple items for sale into one price rather than having the customer select and purchase products separately. Bundling is done by taking products or services that are add-ons to the base product and putting them together in a single offering.

Bundling happens every day in common purchases. Gift baskets of food products are a form of bundling. All-inclusive travel vacations are another. Most of us have experienced bundling at fast-food restaurants. An example of this is the McDonald's Quarter Pounder with Cheese Combo Meal. It comes with a Quarter Pounder with Cheese, medium-sized french fries, and a medium-sized drink. Individually, the items cost more when bought separately. By bundling the items together, McDonald's increases the total amount of the sale, resulting in more revenue.

Price discounting is an effective tool to attract customers and encourage purchases. A discount is a reduction in the listed price for a product or service. A price discount can be temporary, such as a promotional discount to encourage a short-term increase in sales, or longer term, such as a standard customer discount. In business-to-business deals where contracts are involved, the buyer's competitive decision often comes down to the discount rate offered on purchases, even if the competitive price is lower. The discount rate also allows a business to have certainty in managing costs.

There are upsides and downsides to discounting. Care must be taken so that the practice doesn't become predictable or expected by customers. Discounting should have a specific purpose and be carefully thought out before being offered. It's difficult to change a discount once it's been offered. Customers may interpret the end of a discount as an increase in price, which can affect demand.

Pricing for Growth or Profit

How you price depends on your market and the competitive pressures that your business faces. This may be a good time to review Porter's Five Forces of supplier power, customer power, direct competitors, new entrants, and alternatives. That framework describes the factors that influence long-term profitability. Those same factors also help determine pricing strategies.

Pricing pressure will exist when customers have many options from which to choose. In that situation, a strategy that considers competition and value may be appropriate. If direct competition, direct substitutes, or alternatives are not in abundance, then value-based or price-skimming approaches may be more appropriate.

Not all products in a business need to follow the same strategy. You could find that the products or services that bring customers to consider your offerings may need to be priced based on the competition. Simultaneously, accessories could be priced by using a cost-plus model. More advanced services or specialty products within your portfolio could drive more profitability if they are value priced.

In your Strategic Marketing Framework, it's important to specify the pricing strategy or strategies that make sense for your business.

SEGMENT/ PRODUCT LINE Specify targets	LINE 1 Mountain Bikes		LINE 2 Road Bikes		
PEOPLE Identify and describe those you're targeting	USER Bike rider	CUSTOMER Bike rider or parent for younger bikers	USER Biker rider	CUSTOMER Bike rider or parent of younger bikers	
PRODUCT/ FEATURES Identify key products or features for users and customers	Frame type Bike size Aesthetics Component makers	Price Warranty User reviews Personalized bike fitting	Frame material and stiffness Bike size Weight Gear type	Price Warranty Breadth of options Service capability	U P S T R E A M
STRATEGIC MARKETING GOALS What are you trying to achieve?	Drive sales of higher-end mountain bikes and accessories Be seen as the <region> expert on mountain biking		Become the leader in road bike sales in the region Be the community hub for road bike activities (engagement)		
COMPETITION Who are you up against?	Online (Amazon, eBay) Bikes R Us (within 20 mi) REI Academy Outdoors		Online (Amazon, eBay) Bikes R Us (within 20 mi) Walmart, Target, Academy Outdoors		
PRICE POSITION Ideal position vs. competition or price strategy	Entry level bikes—price to big box Pro-level bikes—price skimming Accessories—cost-plus (40% GM target) Coaching and classes— value based		Entry level bikes—price to big box Pro-level bikes—price skimming Accessories—cost-plus (40% GM target) Custom fittings—value-based ($50/hr)		

Figure 10.1 Bike price position example

Key takeaways from this chapter:

1. Customer perception of value is directly influenced by the price of a product or service.
2. Numerous pricing strategies exist. Selecting the appropriate method for your offering, based on customer segmentation, can significantly affect profitability.
3. Pricing can have a direct effect on demand. A low price might lead to increased demand but may negatively affect profit due to reduced margins. Conversely, an excessively high price can decrease demand and subsequently lower profit due to lost sales.
4. The fluctuation in demand as a result of pricing changes is referred to as "demand elasticity."
5. Bundling entails combining multiple products for sale as a single package, potentially leading to a higher average transaction price.
6. Discounting, or offering a reduction in the listed price of a product or service, can be an effective strategy for attracting customers and stimulating sales.

CHAPTER 11

The Marketing Funnel

In this chapter, we'll delve deeper into the marketing funnel. As you may recall from the earlier chapter, the marketing funnel describes the customer's journey toward purchasing goods or services. It's often called the "purchase funnel" because it describes how a customer:

- Finds information about a business
- Considers whether to use that business's goods or services
- Purchases the goods and services
- Establishes a relationship with the company after the purchase of the goods or services
- Evaluates whether the customer feels good enough about the company to become its advocate and encourage other prospective customers to purchase from it

A surefire way of determining whether a customer has become an advocate is whether the person writes a positive review online. Five stars on Yelp, for example, would be valuable to the business. Two stars, however, indicate the possibility of an issue requiring attention. A positive review boosts the business, amplifying your messaging. A negative review detracts from your messaging and may add additional cost or effort to recruiting prospective customers. However, negative reviews may also help a company if they can provide important insight into what areas of the business they should consider improving.

The marketing funnel version we'll use here is a common one comprising five major phases:

- Awareness
- Consideration
- Conversion
- Loyalty
- Advocacy

In some marketing funnels, you will see the consideration phase broken into two different stages: interest and consideration. This provides a more granular analysis. For simplicity, however, we will focus on the funnel's five major phases.

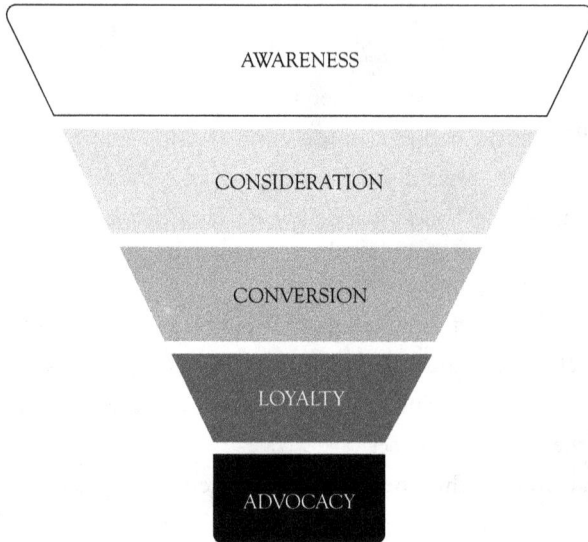

Figure 11.1 The marketing funnel

We're going to apply the marketing funnel to our ice cream shop example.

For somebody to come to the ice cream shop, they have to know that it exists. How do we make them aware? Should we use Instagram pictures? Can we post ads on Facebook? Do we put an ad in a local paper? All of these are ways to drive awareness. Once customers are aware of our ice cream shop, the next step is to get them to consider a visit. Maybe the ice cream shop could have a theme night. Or we could provide some coupons to entice them to consider visiting. We could offer a promotion that would provide customers with two ice cream sandwiches for the price of one. These different tactics don't always happen at the same time. Sometimes a specific ad or message is intended only to drive awareness. A different ad or message can be used later to drive consideration.

Once we have made a customer aware of our business and have gotten them to walk in the door or to contact us, how do we get them to purchase an ice cream sandwich? And beyond purchasing the sandwich, how do we increase the total dollars they spend at the store? Your marketing strategy should be set up to encourage these types of customer behavior.

Once customers have completed their purchases, how do we encourage them to come back? Do we give them a loyalty card, for example, which ultimately will result in a free ice cream sandwich? Do we collect e-mail addresses so we can engage them online, requesting feedback?

You should ask: What level of customer advocacy can we encourage? A positive online review? Spreading the word on social media? If you have collected positive feedback, you should consider asking the respondents if you can share it in your advertising or other messaging.

Let's do a further breakdown of each of the marketing funnel's components.

Awareness

Think about the events and activities that drive awareness of brands and products. They can include marketing campaigns, social events, advertising, content creation, social media posts, messages on websites, and search engine results. All of these will drive awareness, but they don't have to be just advertising and messaging. Some things that drive awareness might not be obvious.

If you've ever watched an NFL game on TV, you'll notice that many of the coaches are using Microsoft Surface tablets on the sidelines. The Microsoft logo is on the back of those devices, and announcers talk about the Microsoft Surface as they're showing coaches sketching out plays. This is a conscious strategy by Microsoft to drive awareness of its product and brand.

Consideration

Customer consideration is an evaluation by a prospective customer about whether to make a purchase from or engage with a company. Driving consideration requires a multipronged strategy derived from our message map. We start by highlighting some of the most important messages that we've identified as valuable to prospective customers. This is also a phase in which proof points become essential in encouraging people to make a purchase or take another type of action that would help the business. Telling prospective customers that the Surface tablets are rugged enough to be used on the sidelines of a football game could encourage customers concerned about the physical resilience of a tablet computer to consider the product for their business.

Conversion

Prospects take the action we hope for during the conversion stage. That action could be purchasing the product or signing an engagement letter for a consulting project. It could be as simple as downloading an e-book. Conversion is not necessarily an actual purchase, although that's what we often use the action to achieve.

In many cases, downloading content, clicking on a YouTube video link, or clicking to view a company commercial during the consideration phase may be measured as a conversion. Still, the ultimate conversion is the purchase of the product or service.

Loyalty

This is the first postpurchase or postconversion phase. The goal is to engage with the new customer on an ongoing basis. It would be a wasted opportunity and a loss of potential future revenue if a single purchase were the only moment you were to engage with the customer—especially after the dollar expenditure by the business to drive awareness, transport the customer through consideration, and encourage the eventual purchase. It is important to focus on building a stronger relationship with the customer in this loyalty phase after the first purchase.

If we secure a customer for our ice cream shop example, our goal should be to cultivate the desire to return to our shop regularly. Routine purchasing is a component of loyalty. But loyalty won't often occur organically. An effective marketing strategy reminds customers to return.

Loyalty could be driven by an e-mail that supplies the customer with a promotion to consider. The hope is that the promotion compels the customer to make future purchases. If that customer regularly comes back to purchase our ice cream, we're successfully managing customer loyalty.

If we're talking about our bike shop, a success in this area could be a customer returning for repairs or to buy new components.

Advocacy

Converting customers into company advocates reduces our marketing expenditures and represents another indicator of a successful marketing strategy.

Word of mouth is among the most effective methods of advocacy. It raises awareness and consideration, and it opens up the possibility for conversion through a purchase.

This type of advocacy costs the business nothing. We cannot stress this enough: if we do a good job managing the conversion and loyalty phases, then our advocates become an incredibly effective means of attracting new customers.

Advocacy also is an essential part of the value equation in that word of mouth references are much more effective than paid marketing. Yet it often is ignored. In fact, it could be argued that the advocacy phase is among the most critical for small- and mid-sized businesses because it's difficult to compete with larger brands and larger companies that have bigger marketing budgets.

Note: Good word of mouth trumps good advertising any day because it may result in lower costs to acquire a customer, which increases the amount of profit we'll make.

Understanding the Intersection of the Marketing Funnel and the Sales Pipeline

In addition to the marketing funnel, most companies also manage their customer opportunities through a sales funnel or pipeline. While the marketing funnel comprises five phases, the sales pipeline focuses on leads, prospects, contacts, and customers. Sales pipeline leads are people who are already in the consideration phase.

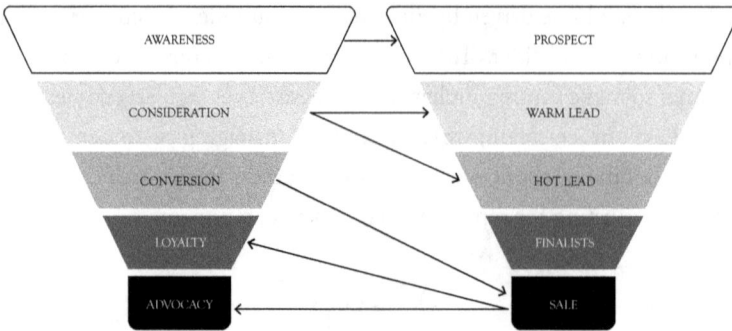

Figure 11.2 Marketing funnel interaction with the sales pipeline

If the marketing team has done a good job in awareness, then the people interested in and engaged with the company will eventually become leads. In the early phase of consideration, they would be a marketing-qualified lead or a warm lead. Once they have engaged more with the company and taken specific actions to indicate that they are serious about purchasing, they become what is known as a sales-qualified lead in the sales pipeline. In this phase, much of the effort moves from marketing to the sales team in order to close the sale.

Managing activities in the marketing funnel and the sales pipeline can help diagnose problems with your marketing efforts. The sales team works with the prospect or the lead until they become a customer. Once they have purchased or signed, they begin moving from the conversion phase into the loyalty phase. Both sales and marketing have roles to play in ensuring happy customers who are loyal and willing to repurchase or recommend the company to others.

If you have a lot of awareness, such as getting many views on a Google or Facebook ad, but no clicks, then there could be a problem with your awareness activities. The prospects aren't moving into the consideration phase.

Why? Was it incorrect targeting in your advertising or your awareness campaign? Is the messaging wrong? Is it possible that your target segments are not responding to the key messages that you selected? Are assumptions about the target segment wrong? If you are doing awareness correctly, you should see engagement based on the awareness activity. On the other hand, if you have a lot of clicks or engagement with your advertising or messaging but not a lot of conversions, this may indicate a problem within the consideration phase.

Why aren't people purchasing the product or contracting for the service? Is the pricing too high? Are the steps to complete the purchase too tricky? If you have a number of customer-purchasing actions that were begun but not completed, it's essential to understand why. There's a term for this customer behavior: "shopping cart abandonment."

If customers buy once but never engage with the company or purchase from the business again, why? Do they go to a competitor? If they buy from you but won't refer you to other customers, it's essential to understand why.

A grocery store where David once worked used flyers advertising offers to drive awareness. The flyers were mailed to people's homes and posted throughout the store.

Customers who entered the store but did not buy any of the items advertised in the flyer demonstrated that the flyers were not achieving the desired outcome. The store wasted money producing the flyers, despite creating awareness. Entering the store meant that the consideration phase had begun. But conversion did not occur. The flyer advertising was ineffective. Worse, the likelihood of that customer ever entering the store again could be pretty low. If the customer didn't purchase something advertised as part of the consideration phase, there was something about the experience that the grocery store needed to address. Otherwise, there would be a potential for more of the same: permanently lost purchases and permanently lost customers. Good management of the marketing funnel and understanding the sales pipeline are critical for maximizing your marketing expenditure and minimizing the loss of your prospective customers.

If done right, the marketing will provide warm and hot leads to the sales team, lure prospective customers to our ice cream shop, or persuade them to contact our bike business to make a purchase. Good marketing enables the sales team or customer-facing employees by increasing the conversion rate. Good management of the funnel also allows you to diagnose potential challenges or weaknesses in your offerings or marketing communications. It will provide you with information to optimize the amount of money spent to make customers aware of your business and cause them to consider your products. Finally, it can also reduce your overall marketing expenses, increase your profit, and deliver more value to the customer.

In the next chapter, we'll talk about communication channels and ways to drive awareness, consideration, and conversion.

Key takeaways from this chapter:

1. The marketing funnel outlines the customer's journey, encompassing the phases before, during, and after the acquisition of a product or service.
2. Although various interpretations of the marketing funnel exist, our preferred version consists of five primary components: Awareness, Consideration, Conversion, Loyalty, and Advocacy.
3. The sales pipeline emphasizes leads, prospects, customers, and contacts, and aligns with the marketing funnel during the Consideration and Conversion stages of the customer journey.

CHAPTER 12

Advertising and Placement—Where and How to Connect to Your Target Customers

Now you can see how understanding your customers informs decisions about what you offer to provide value to prospective customers. You've also discovered the importance of identifying key messages that will resonate with them. And you've come to learn about the journey that most, if not all, customers go through to purchase your product or service. Through your competitive analysis, you've also realized the importance of understanding your competitors' customer messaging.

The next step in the marketing process is getting your key message points to prospective customers. Having a great product with solid messages doesn't do any good if prospective customers never learn about you. How and where you deliver the message is essential. Well-managed advertising and communications can cost-effectively drive customer purchase activity, but poorly managed approaches can be expensive and drag on profitability. Well-executed marketing communications can generate more profit by minimizing spending on messaging and advertising that doesn't result in sales or service contracts.

Marketing messages can be delivered to prospective customers in several ways. Historical channels included print, television, and direct mail. Digital channels have become more prevalent during the past 15 years or so. These include social media sites, search engines such as Google and Bing, and third-party websites. These channels can present information about your company either as advertising or as information, otherwise known as content. The manner in which you transmit your messaging affects costs and revenues.

If we use the example of a newspaper, two traditional ways exist to communicate messages to prospective customers. One would be to buy an ad in the paper. The second would be to persuade the paper to publish a review or a story about your company.

Acquiring a new customer through a paid ad naturally reduces the company's profit as it is a cost that you need to pay. A review or story costs nothing, so profit is higher using this customer-acquisition strategy.

A newspaper ad is an example of "paid media messaging." Coverage of your product or service obtained without direct company expenditure is considered "organic media messaging." A good review that communicates some of the key messages about your business is considered organic messaging.

The money a business spends to obtain a new customer is called the customer acquisition cost (CAC). CAC is calculated by dividing the cost of sales and marketing by the number of customers acquired. If it costs $500 to run an ad that attracts 50 customers, the CAC for that ad is $10 per customer. To calculate CAC for a product line or across the sales and marketing spectrum of ads, salespeople, and digital marketing, the calculation would be the entire cost of sales and marketing. A salesperson at $75,000 a year and a marketing budget of $50,000 per year would translate to a sales and marketing cost of $125,000. If the result was 50 new customers for the year, the CAC would be $125,000 divided by 50 for a $2,500 CAC. That's not too bad if you are selling a $100,000 car, but not great if you are selling a $5,000 computer. Understanding CAC is crucial to tuning the efficacy of your sales and marketing efforts. Measuring CAC and working to improve costs while increasing new customer acquisition is a good way to tune your marketing and drive profitability.

We touched on the marketing framework that helps plan for effectively delivering messages in Chapter 3 when we introduced the POEM (paid, earned, and owned media) model.

To recap: owned media channels represent those we control and on which we can communicate to prospective customers directly. These include your company website, e-mail list, LinkedIn business profile, Twitter account, and Instagram account. Communicating messages through these channels to reach prospective customers costs the company nothing.

Paid media channels, on the other hand, require the company to pay a fee for sharing information. Google Ads, Facebook Ads, and LinkedIn post boosting are examples of paid channels. One advantage of paid channels is that they typically supply data-analytic tools to enable targeting specific prospective customer groups.

For example, you may target customer groups using demographic categories, including:

- Age
- Language
- Gender
- Education level, field of study, or school attended
- Industry, job level, or employer
- Location

Prospective customers also may be targeted according to interests, such as:

- Entertainment preferences (favorite actors, musicians, or movie genres)
- Fitness and wellness (diet types, nutrition protocols, favorite forms of exercise, or other health regimens)
- Food and drink (cooking styles, types of meals, or favorite restaurants)
- Hobbies and activities (current events, travel, or photography)
- Fashion and design (clothing, accessories, or styles)
- Sports and outdoors (hiking, fishing, rock climbing, or professional teams)
- Technology (computers, software, or smartphones)

This type of targeting is powerful because it enables spending money only on the prospective customers you choose. It reduces the risk that you are paying for advertising seen by those who have a low likelihood of ever becoming a paying customer.

Paid-channel data analytics reveal advertising and messaging performance. That information may be mapped to the marketing funnel.

Impressions 21,236	Clicks 1552	Click-Through Rate (CTR) 0.73
Cost ($1152)	Avg. Cost Per Click (CPC) .70	Conversions 93
Conversion Rate .06		

Figure 12.1 Digital advertising performance dashboard example

This online performance dashboard example shows a little over 21,000 views or impressions (awareness) of an ad that occurred during the reporting period. Viewers who clicked on ads looking for more information (consideration) totaled slightly over 1,500 of those viewers. Finally, 93 actual purchases or desired events (conversion) happened.

The dashboard shows that the cost per click (CPC) was $0.70. It also shows that the click-through rate (CTR) was 0.73 percent. That means that around 7 percent of ad views resulted in a click. While this CTR may seem low, it provides insight into how the messaging is performing. Paid platforms usually provide CTR- and CPC-rate information to help ascertain messaging performance relative to the overall channel.

Paid messaging and advertising work similarly, regardless of channel. For example, LinkedIn, Instagram, and Twitter post boosts, as well as Google display ads or Google search ads, provide comparable targeting and reporting options.

The "earned" channel is the last component of the POEM framework. This is where others spread the company's messaging at no expense to the company. The company "earns" the sharing of your messaging by others.

Word-of-mouth advertising is an excellent example of earned media. A customer leaving a positive review on Yelp or Google is earned media. A press article that talks about the company or product is earned media. It's particularly potent if the writer picks up a company's key messages and shares them with their publication's audience. Earned media is effective due to its impact on potential customers and because it costs a business nothing. Yet it yields more customers and revenue.

Content Versus Advertising

There is a lot of confusion about the difference between content marketing and advertising. It need not be so difficult to understand. Think about the POEM framework. Content marketing delivers your messages in a way that will encourage sharing from readers or viewers while also driving awareness of your company and your messaging. An interesting and shareable blog post will drive awareness by getting the company's message in front of prospective customers at no additional cost to the company. Ticketbud, an Austin-based event ticketing company, wrote a blog post titled "SXSW Hacks to Hosting a Kick-A$$ Event," which was widely shared as a social media link that landed readers on the Ticketbud website. This is a great example of earned media because everyone who clicked the link was a visitor that Ticketbud didn't have to pay an advertiser to get.

Advertising delivers your messages through paid channels, such as television, radio, print, or digital channels, such as social media ads or display advertising. It is rarely shared among readers and viewers, while content marketing is designed to be shared.

Content marketing includes editorials, educational articles, e-books, videos, online courses, or webinars that provide subject matter likely to be interesting to prospective customers in your target market segments. It can be educational, informative, or entertaining. Content marketing is developed specifically to drive awareness and consideration of your brand through earned media.

Creating Ad Campaigns

Campaigns are short-term bundles of promotions, advertising, and content pieces that drive a desired outcome or event. In our bike business example, the company could decide to create a campaign to drive bike sales before school concludes for summer break.

Rather than just running random ads or publishing content haphazardly, campaigns allow the development of marketing materials (ads and content) that work in concert to create awareness of the business and drive consideration and sales (conversions). Designing a campaign around a theme such as "Summer Biking Fun" would be a way to focus your messaging and drive cost-effective sales. The ad and content messaging would incorporate the words or images linked to the theme.

Hypothesis development and A/B testing are particularly helpful concepts to be aware of in developing ads and campaigns. We encourage you to explore this area once you have built your marketing strategy and begun implementing it.

Marketing professionals don't create ads and content without purpose. They have specific goals in mind. A goal could be to "increase the number of visits to the store by highlighting our in-store individualized service and product line breadth." It could be to "achieve a 25 percent increase in store website purchases by communicating our checkout process benefits." Or it might be to "drive family or group visits by developing ads and content around shared fun in our ice cream store."

The marketing goal sets the objective for the ads or campaigns. However, executives develop effective advertising and content through a marketing hypothesis. The hypothesis approach starts with a statement. Then A/B testing is done to select the best-performing ad content over a period of time. The hypothesis is something that can be created and tested.

A/B testing is a method used by marketers in which they develop two ads that are run in paid marketing channels. Marketers determine which ad generates the most effective response. That ad will continue. The other would be replaced with another ad to be tested against the remaining ad.

Let's go back to the ice cream store example. If the marketing goal is to "drive family or group visits by developing ads and content around shared fun in our ice cream store," the hypothesis statement could be: "Incorporating images of people enjoying our ice cream sandwiches together will increase click-through rate by 15 percent."

To conduct an A/B test, we could develop two ads with identical copies but with different images. One image would depict an ice cream sandwich by itself. The other would depict a person eating and enjoying the ice cream sandwich. We would run those ads for, say, two weeks. Then, we'd analyze the results by looking at the data analytics provided by the platform on which we ran the ads. The more effective ad, based on the number of impressions and clicks, would continue to run. We'd replace the other ad with a new one. That revised ad would include some type of change, such as a new message or a different image. Each time that the A/B test is run, only one element at a time should change, and the lower-performing ad would be replaced with a new test ad.

It is critical in A/B testing that only one element of the ad should be changed at a time, be it the image or an element in the text. This clarifies what is working and what is not. It enables us to improve the ad with concrete, causal data.

As you develop and implement your advertising and content marketing, it is imperative to quickly test what causes a response. It's equally important to be cautious about spending a lot of money on advertising or content placement until you know that the materials you have developed are driving the results you seek.

A good approach in marketing is to move quickly in developing and refining your advertising and content but spend slowly. Remember, the goal of the value equation is to acquire customers at the lowest possible cost, which maximizes profit.

Creating Content for Social and Viral Marketing

A significant opportunity exists for businesses to get word-of-mouth or earned awareness through social media. Because your social media pages are media channels owned by your business, the cost to your company typically is zero.

Social media sites such as Facebook, Instagram, Twitter, TikTok, and YouTube are optimal for sharing content about your business. Other social media sites are tailored to specific audiences. LinkedIn, for example, is for business professionals, while Nextdoor focuses on neighborhoods.

Two metrics commonly used to gauge these sites' audiences are monthly active users and monthly unique visitors. These metrics can help you understand the potential reach of your content.

Not all sites are appropriate for every business. It's essential to concentrate on the sites used by your target market, which the market segmentation exercise helps you identify. To be effective in social media, you want to create content that is useful and meaningful to your target customer. Most importantly, you must create content that people want to share with others.

Shared content brings enormous value to your business. It results in earned views. You didn't pay for those views, and you didn't directly send that content; others did it on your behalf. Rapidly shared content by a large number of social media users also is known as "viral" content. Viral content depicting your business provides high levels of awareness at no cost.

The Strategic Marketing Framework

Using the concepts and information we've discussed in this chapter, we're able to complete the Strategic Marketing Goals, Promotions/Campaigns, and Placement sections of the Strategic Marketing Framework.

SEGMENT/ PRODUCT LINE Specify targets	LINE 1 Mountain Bikes		LINE 2 Road Bikes		
PEOPLE Identify and describe those you're targeting	USER Bike rider	CUSTOMER Bike rider or parent for younger bikers	USER Bike rider	CUSTOMER Bike rider or parent of younger bikers	
PRODUCT/ FEATURES Identify and describe those you're targeting	Frame type Bike size Aesthetics Component makers	Price Warranty User reviews Personalized bike fitting	Frame material and stiffness Bike size Weight Gear type	Price Warranty Breadth of options Service capability	U P S T R E A M
STRATEGIC MARKETING GOALS What are you trying to achieve?	Drive sales of higher-end mountain bikes and accessories Be seen as the <region> expert on mountain biking		Become the leader in road bike sales in the region Be the community hub for road bike activities (engagement)		
COMPETITION Who are you up against?	Online (Amazon, eBay) Bikes R Us (within 20 mi) REI Academy Outdoors		Online (Amazon, eBay) Bikes R Us (within 20 mi) Walmart, Target, Academy Outdoors		

PRICE POSITION Ideal position vs. competition or price strategy					
KEY MESSAGES What matters to users/customers	*Local—here to serve* *Top brands—available in store* *Expert mountain bike staff* *Competitively priced*		*Local—here to serve* *Guaranteed fit—in-store fitting* *Preferred Partner to local clubs* *Top brands—competitively priced*		D O
PROMOTIONS/ CAMPAIGNS Get creative	*Attack the mountain like a pro*		*The authority on <region> road biking*		W N S T
PLACEMENT Where you will run campaigns	DIGITAL *Facebook, Instagram Mountain-bike.com Google*	TRADITIONAL *Local newspaper MTB club visits MTB pop-ups at local trails*	DIGITAL *Facebook, Instagram, YouTube Cycling .com Google*	TRADITIONAL *Local newspaper Host weekly bike rides In-store fittings School sponsorships*	R E A M

Figure 12.2 Promotion and placement example for the bike business

The main goals of your marketing strategy go in the strategic marketing goal section. We recommend limiting the total number of goals to three. More than that results in confusion when developing marketing messages and creative content.

The key messages you identified earlier support your strategic goals. Key messages influence those goals. Remember: you should feel free to update framework sections based on market or competitive changes. Making the framework a living document enables you to see how each of the elements works together and drives your overall market strategy.

In this chapter, we also added the promotions/campaigns that you will use to drive key messages to your target audiences. All of your content and advertising should lead a prospective user to see your business and brand in the way you intend.

When we refer to "placement" in the Four Ps model, we are talking about the channels of reaching the prospective customer. The channels for placement comprise two streams: the digital channels and the traditional and non-digital marketing activities. Examples of these types of channels include:

Traditional Media

Print media—newspapers and magazines
Broadcast media—radio and TV
Direct mail—catalogs, brochures, and mailers
Outdoor advertising—flyers, billboards, and signs
Telemarketing—surveys, info calls

Digital Media

Websites—Topic-specific websites and blogs
Social media sites—Facebook, Twitter, Yelp, Instagram, and YouTube
Search engine marketing—Google, Yahoo, and Bing
Video ads—YouTube and TikTok
E-mail marketing—MailChimp and Constant Contact

Key takeaways from this chapter:

1. Marketing messages can be disseminated to customers through traditional (print, television, outdoor, and direct mail) and digital (search engines, social media, websites, and e-mail) channels.

2. Advertising expenditure is a cost that influences profitability. The customer acquisition cost (CAC) refers to the total amount a company spends to acquire a new customer.

3. Refining your messaging and delivery channels to decrease the CAC directly affects profitability.

4. Content marketing conveys your message in a manner that promotes sharing among readers or viewers, often through social media platforms.

5. Advertising disseminates messages through paid channels.

6. A/B testing is a technique employed to assess and enhance advertisements, thereby boosting performance over time.

CHAPTER 13

Customer Relationship Management Tools

By now, you should be very familiar with both the value equation and the marketing funnel. As you know from the value equation, your goal should be to see your revenue grow at the lowest cost possible. We've also shared the importance of building customer loyalty and a long-term relationship with your customers. It's estimated that acquiring a new customer can be five to seven times more expensive than keeping an existing customer.

Strong customer loyalty also reveals what's going right or wrong before the impact on your business becomes significant. Loyal customers are more willing to tell you what isn't working. First-time or transactional customers frequently won't. They simply don't return. Building a solid relationship with your customers is essential. That's true whether you have a traditionally transactional business like a retail store or a service business that is more relationship based, such as a consulting firm.

Customer relationship development, loyalty, and return purchases don't happen by accident. They take effort and an investment of both time and energy. It's worth it. The payoff is a customer who costs less to engage over time but results in more purchases over the lifetime of the business–customer relationship.

Smart businesses put effort into formalizing their customer relationship management (CRM) efforts using CRM tools.

What Is a CRM Tool?

Before computers became a routine part of running a company, businesspeople managed relationships with Rolodexes and business cards. There were specially designed products that facilitated adding important customer information to Rolodex cards. Three-ring binder books with clear plastic business card inserts were common. They enabled information to be read from notes taken on the backs of business cards. Over time, paper planners incorporated tools for scheduling and noting follow-up reminders with prospective or existing customers. While many businesses still manage their customers this way, others are using CRM software platforms that manage the relationships between your business and its customers.

The first software-based management tools moved the business card contact information onto the computer. The invention of contact management tools in the 1980s provided quick access to information and note updates on hundreds or thousands of customers.

Today's CRM tools go well beyond contact management and note-taking. They integrate marketing, shipping, accounting, and scheduling software to provide information about the entire customer journey. They also guide customers through the marketing and sales funnels. When used well, CRM tools result in continued contact with customers, yield information about the value or profitability of specific customers, and optimize marketing based on each customer's needs and location on the customer journey. If you aren't using CRM software, your competitors almost certainly are.

Types of CRM Tools

Not all CRM tools are the same nor are all types appropriate or necessary for a small- or mid-sized business. CRMs are meant to be integrated into the operational life of your business. The right CRM for you is the one that you use regularly. Just like e-mail and cell phone use, it only works well if it's incorporated into your workflow and makes your job more manageable over time. Not all CRMs will suit you and your business. Some investigation, testing, and trial use will be necessary.

There are three primary CRM categories:

- Operational
- Collaborative
- Analytical

An operational CRM manages and tracks your company's interactions with your prospects and customers and helps automate and track customer communications, marketing activities, the sales process, and service/support activities. A CRM of this type integrates and automates the information among these three functional areas to provide a holistic view of the activity with specific prospects and customers. The sales process management component of an operational CRM helps the sales team in pipeline management. It can assist in generating and converting leads into customers. Many operational CRMs include the ability to integrate with other in-house systems, such as billing, shipping, and inventory systems. Operational CRMs are the most commonly used by small- and mid-sized businesses.

Larger organizations with many divisions, locations, distribution channel partners, or logistics partners generally use a collaborative CRM that integrates with other software platforms to make cross-organization management of prospects or customers more efficient. These types of CRMs integrate information from and about customers, partners, suppliers, and distributors. While collaborative CRMs are essential for large, distributed organizations, they may be too complicated or challenging to implement in a smaller business. The goal of a CRM is to improve the ability to capture value by increasing efficiency, not to add more work to already busy lives.

An analytical CRM takes information from existing in-house systems and organizes and analyzes data from sales, marketing, and customer service to provide information for better decision making. In many cases, an analytical CRM can bring together information from disparate sources to provide an integrated view of customer engagement. Typically, analytical CRMs pull data from existing systems to create a data warehouse that enables analysis and reporting. Analytical CRMs are great if you already have existing marketing, sales, and support systems and want to integrate customer data to improve operational efficiency.

The Benefits of Using a CRM

A well-implemented CRM improves engagement with past, current, and prospective customers. It also helps with the overall management of a business and provides insights for making ongoing changes to remain competitive and profitable. CRM benefits include the ability to:

- Track relationship information about prospects and customers
- Track activity and transactions by prospects and customers
- Improve the sales teams' ability to close deals by providing more complete information
- Optimize customer service effectiveness
- Track marketing communications with prospects and users
- Understand purchases and services to specific customers over time
- Provide a comprehensive view of customer engagement with the company

Even the most basic use of a CRM will allow you to build lists of customers' and prospects' communication preferences. These lists can be used to deliver targeted marketing messages and promotions. This information is vital because your contact lists from a CRM are among the most valuable owned media channels. Many businesses, unfortunately, ignore this aspect of CRMs.

Effective CRM use allows a business to communicate with prospects and customers, track customer activity, and optimize interactions—all of which improve company marketing efforts.

Marketing Automation Tools

Many transactional businesses, such as restaurants and retail stores, don't need a complete CRM with sales pipeline and service tracking. A marketing automation tool might be more than enough to optimize the business's marketing activities.

Many CRMs provide marketing automation tools that can be used without the rest of the CRM features. You may expand the use of the CRM's other features on an as-needed basis.

Marketing automation refers to software platforms and technologies designed for marketing departments and organizations to market through multiple channels online more effectively and efficiently. This reduces the overall labor and costs of running marketing campaigns.

Replacing high-touch, repetitive manual processes with automated solutions reduces costs. That translates to higher value, or profit, captured by the organization—which is another example of the value equation at work.

Marketing automation platforms provide dashboards that marketers can use to plan, manage, and measure all of their marketing activities and campaigns, online and offline. They automate the customer's journey through the marketing funnel by managing activity to convert leads into customers.

A marketing automation platform can also track the behavior of prospective customers on social media, in e-mail, and with websites to understand their journey through the marketing funnel. This tracking yields market intelligence on responses by prospective customers to specific ads or campaigns.

Choosing between a CRM or a marketing automation tool depends on the needs of your business. What activities are most important? Managing customer relationships? Marketing campaign tracking? Round-the-clock access to customer information?

Rank the offered services. Determine which ones appear best for you. Then test different types of tools before deciding. Most platforms offer free trial versions of their services.

CRM and marketing automation management platforms can be important tools in your toolbox for reducing costs and maximizing your marketing effectiveness.

Key takeaways from this chapter:

1. The cost of acquiring new customers is substantially higher than retaining existing, satisfied customers.
2. Establishing robust relationships with your clientele is crucial.
3. Customer relationship management (CRM) tools aid in managing customer relations while offering analytical insights into your business's performance.

(Continues)

(Continued)

4. Utilizing CRM effectively enables businesses to engage with prospects and customers, monitor activities, and optimize interactions with both prospects and existing clients.

5. Marketing automation platforms have been developed to facilitate more efficient and effective marketing across multiple online channels.

CHAPTER 14

Metrics That Matter

How do you know if your marketing strategy is working? Ensuring you get results is the final step of building out the Strategic Marketing Framework. A famous and widely debated business maxim states, "If you can't measure it, you can't manage it." Variations of this mantra include "If you don't measure it, then you can't improve it." Both axioms present a fundamental truth: to know whether your business strategy is having its intended effect, you need to know your starting point and how you are progressing.

From a business perspective, the point of measuring things is to create more happy customers and increase profits. With that in mind, companies should not ignore the recent shift in consumer sentiment around mission-driven companies. More consumers today are willing to pay higher prices—and founders/executives are willing to accept lower profits—if the companies are doing well. And, like other businesses, mission-driven companies benefit from measuring to ensure that progress is being made toward the mission goals. The metrics you select should always help answer important broader questions:

- Are sales growing?
- Are customers returning to purchase again?
- Are your products and services delivering what customers expect or want?
- Are customers becoming references for your business?
- Is the business generating a profit and a positive cash flow (more money coming in than going out after all expenses are paid)?

These sample metrics are a mere subset of the huge number of ways marketing teams obtain information regarding the state of the business and any changes that may be needed. Metrics are gauges that allow marketers to "tune" strategy to build a growing, profitable business.

Establishing baseline metrics is the first step: Where are you in your business *before* you start tracking your metrics?

You need this information before making any major changes to your strategic framework. Baseline metrics should also be done at the beginning of an advertising campaign or a sales promotion and anytime you take actions that you hope will improve outcomes.

For example, if we run a two-for-one coupon weekend promotion at the ice cream shop, we'd want to know average weekend sales and sales for the weekend prior to the start of the promotion. This information would provide a baseline understanding of what sales looked like before we ran the promotion.

If we found that sales stayed the same or increased only a couple of percentage points during the promotion, we'd need to consider whether the extra cost of providing free ice cream was returning any value.

Baseline metrics also help in setting realistic goals. The absence of baseline metrics typically results in unrealistic or irrelevant goals. Baseline metrics also reveal business areas requiring attention within the marketing strategy and its execution.

Track for Improvement, Not Numbers

It's important to measure things that are essential to improving business performance. The value equation helps management think about things that improve customer satisfaction and profitability.

Unfortunately, measuring useless things occurs all the time. Measuring page views or impressions of a digital ad or a video ad is helpful in analyzing whether the placement of your digital ad or content is resulting in it being presented to people. But if the page views or impressions aren't resulting in clicks to your website or purchases of your product, then the page view metric isn't useful on its own. It's not uncommon to invest more money in digital advertising because it appears that the page views or impressions are growing but not resulting in additional sales. Page views and impressions are not sales; they are measures of how many people have seen the advertising. If the page views and impressions are not leading to a higher rate of sales, then spending more money on the ads is likely not going to result in increased profit. If anything, it may result in increased costs and decreased profit because you are spending money on advertising that is not resulting in sales. Measuring the things that matter and ensuring that they are leading to the ultimate result desired, usually sales, is essential.

Choosing Metrics

It can be confusing to decide which metrics are best to manage a business, particularly when so many exist. Some metrics are appropriate for a particular business function. Some measure activity at a granular level, such as hourly sales volume. Others measure outcomes at a broad level, such as revenue or market share growth. They provide information useful for investors and senior executives but are of limited benefit to improving the marketing strategy.

The value equation provides a map of where metrics-enhancing marketing activities may be used on both sides of the equation: value creation and value capture.

Some metrics, such as the Net Promoter Score and Customer Lifetime Value, require more action and time to collect. They should be reviewed monthly, quarterly, or annually. Some metrics, like cost per impression and conversion rate, provide an idea of how the marketing activities and business are performing in real time. Information yielded in such areas often reveals operational changes that should be made.

All these metrics have online calculators and formulas. Rather than overwhelm readers with numbers and mathematical formulas, we'll provide an overview of these metrics and their use.

Value Creation Metrics

Conversions are the completed desired events or transactions for the period being measured. In many cases, this desired event is a sale with resulting revenue, but it can also be some other action. For a nonprofit organization, the conversion could be a donation, or it could be someone signing up for volunteer hours. Conversions indicate the end of a

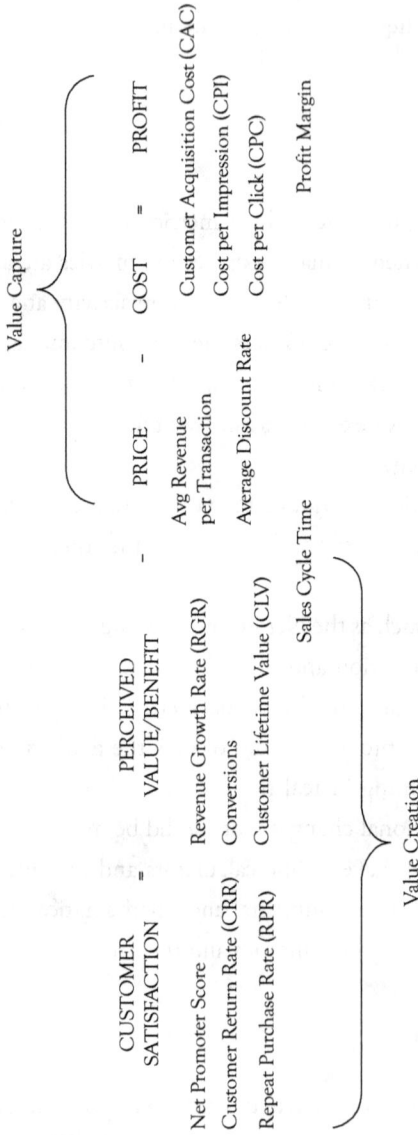

$$\underset{\text{SATISFACTION}}{\text{CUSTOMER}} = \underset{\text{VALUE/BENEFIT}}{\text{PERCEIVED}} - \text{PRICE} - \text{COST} = \text{PROFIT}$$

Value Creation:
- Net Promoter Score
- Customer Return Rate (CRR)
- Repeat Purchase Rate (RPR)
- Revenue Growth Rate (RGR)
- Conversions
- Customer Lifetime Value (CLV)
- Sales Cycle Time

Price:
- Avg Revenue per Transaction
- Average Discount Rate

Value Capture / Cost / Profit:
- Customer Acquisition Cost (CAC)
- Cost per Impression (CPI)
- Cost per Click (CPC)
- Profit Margin

Figure 14.1 Metrics for managing the value equation

prospect's consideration phase and the completion of the action desired by the marketer.

Conversion measurements vary according to functional business needs. Daily purchase totals, for example, may be the best metric for restaurants or service businesses that run on individual transactions. That measurement then may be used to determine a metric such as the average revenue per transaction.

To understand the flow from impressions to clicks to conversions in digital marketing activities, the total of conversions is a particularly useful metric. That measurement also reveals how effective the upper end of the marketing funnel is in driving the rate of conversion.

As discussed in Chapter 2, net promoter score (NPS) is a widely used metric that shows customer loyalty and advocacy. Using a proprietary formula, it computes the ratio of promoters, passive customers, and detractors for your business, product, or brand into a single numeric indicator.

Customer return rate measures your company's customer loyalty. Businesses with an e-commerce component using customer e-mail addresses or login accounts are able to track activity and return rates online. Traditional brick-and-mortar and transactional businesses, such as bars and restaurants, also may track customer return rates by using tools such as loyalty cards and point-of-sale systems that match customers with their credit card numbers.

Repeat purchase rate is similar to the customer return rate, except it measures the repeat purchase of specific products or services. This metric helps marketers understand which products are generating return customers. While the repeat purchase rate can be helpful to most businesses, for more transactional operations such as our ice cream shop, it can also help determine which products are popular so that we can trim offerings that customers are ignoring.

Revenue growth rate (RGR) measures the change in revenue over a period of time. Many companies measure revenue growth rates on a weekly, quarterly, and annual basis. For example, a weekly revenue growth rate calculation measures the change in revenue from the previous week. If last week's ice cream sales were $3,800 and this week's sales were $4,200, then the weekly revenue growth rate would be 10.5 percent. However, if the weekly sales numbers were reversed, then the

RGR would be –9.5 percent. Our revenue would be declining week over week, and we would want to try to understand why.

Customer lifetime value (CLV) analyzes an average customer's revenue generated over the entire relationship with a company. CLV reveals the value of customers to a company over time. It's often paired with customer acquisition cost (CAC) to determine the profitability of a customer over time. It also underscores the importance of generating return customer visits. Let's say the average customer for the ice cream shop buys two ice cream sandwiches for $10 and comes in once a month. Let's also say the average lifespan of a customer is two years. Then the CLV of the customer is $240. If the gross margin for our product is 30 percent, then that customer's average gross margin value is $72. Decisions about marketing and advertising spending can be made more intelligently when you know the CLV.

Value Capture Metrics

Sales cycle time spans the value creation and value capture aspects of the value equation. It measures the time from the first engagement with a prospective customer to the sale or conversion action. Sales cycle time provides insights into what changes may be needed to shorten the time from consideration to conversion in the marketing funnel.

Average revenue is an important metric in general for marketing people. It can be measured per transaction (also known as average order value or AOV), which indicates the average total sale of a customer's purchase. Think about McDonald's. If the average revenue per transaction is $14.50, it can be compared across days—for example, by asking if the average revenue per transaction is higher on Fridays than on Tuesdays—or across stores, or at different times of the year. This is helpful in putting together promotions and bundling strategies to drive higher transaction averages on days with lower averages. This type of revenue averaging may also be calculated as average revenue per user (ARPU), which would measure the typical customer revenue average. This is helpful for understanding how customer growth or higher ARPU would affect revenue and profitability. Not to confuse you too much, but another way to measure average revenue is an approach often used for businesses that have products with add-on options: average revenue per unit. It is helpful for businesses such as cable services that measure average revenue per home (unit) and mobile phone companies that measure the average amount of revenue that each mobile phone gets from cellular service and add-on features.

All of these are simply forms of measuring the average revenue. It's calculated by dividing the total revenue by the number of customers or units. Let's take our ice cream store example. If our revenue for the day was $2,573 and we had 210 customers, then our average revenue per customer was $12.25. But let's assume that we were doing catering. Another way we could look at this would be to divide the revenue by the number of transactions. Maybe the $2,573 is composed of 15 catering orders. Then our average revenue per transaction would be $171.53. You should be able to see that increasing daily sales by one new catering order has more impact on the daily revenue than getting 10 new customers to come to the store. This level of analysis lets you focus your marketing efforts on ways to maximize the return for your efforts.

Average discount rate is a measure that indicates what the average rate of discount is across all of your transactions. It is most appropriate for businesses where discounting is used to increase consideration and generate conversions.

As we shared in Chapter 12, CAC shows how much your business spends on gaining a customer. The longer you keep a customer or the larger the transaction size, the more you can spend on marketing to acquire that customer. You don't want to spend a lot of money to acquire a customer who doesn't generate a profitable transaction. Spending $10 to acquire a customer who is going to buy a $30 meal that generates a gross profit of $6 doesn't make a lot of sense. However, spending that amount for a high-end restaurant where the customer will spend $100 or more makes perfect sense.

Cost per impression is a digital-marketing metric that measures how much each ad impression costs. It's also a part of the marketing funnel. The more impressions at a low price, the more effective you could say your marketing is for the Awareness section of the funnel.

Cost per click measures the cost of a prospect taking an action that leads to consideration. Think about it as a prospective customer: you see an ad on a website or Facebook and click on it to read more. That click means that you are potentially interested in the product or service. Some digital marketing channels provide the opportunity for companies to advertise with them to pay by impression or by click. When submitting ads on Google, for example, you have the option of selecting a cost-per-click or cost-per-impression bid. You will pay Google based on what you select and what the desired results are from placing the ad in the Google display network. Paying for impressions means that you pay for the number of times that an ad is displayed for users to see. Paying for clicks means that you only pay each time a user clicks a link in your ad (an action). There are more impressions that result in no action. So, the cost that a business pays for clicks typically is more than what it pays for impressions because the channel is charging only for ads that result in a customer taking a specific action to engage with your company.

Profit margin is the ultimate value capture metric. At the end of the day, you want to maximize your margin or the amount of money you make after paying all expenses. That is the economic value that you capture.

Measuring your marketing activities helps you understand what is working and what isn't. There are a great number of metrics used by marketers. The important thing to remember is that metrics are valuable only when they are used to understand how your business is doing and help you identify the things that are and are not working.

The goal isn't just to have an effective strategy but also to generate efficient execution. That leads to optimized marketing costs. Effective and efficient market execution improves the profitability of firms by maximizing revenue while minimizing marketing expenses.

Key takeaways from this chapter:

1. Quantitative measurements, or metrics, play a pivotal role in determining the efficacy of your marketing strategy.
2. By setting a baseline for each metric, you can better assess the impact of the actions implemented.
3. Use metrics to monitor progress and enhance outcomes, rather than merely recording performance.
4. Select metrics that are closely aligned with the specific marketing initiatives being undertaken.

CHAPTER 15

Summary

If you have built your strategic framework as you've read each of this book's chapters, you now should have a structured outline of your company's marketing strategy.

To know whether your strategy is working, simply use the value equation. Are you generating the profit you planned? Is your customer base growing? Are your customers satisfied? These are generic questions that can be measured. But there are more basic ways to know if your market strategy is on the right track.

One is whether sales are growing. You should see an increase in sales beyond your previous rate. If you see an increase, your marketing is likely beginning to work. If you don't see an increase, you should begin investigating. Is it your pricing? Are you missing something that customers want regarding product or service features? What part of your strategy is not working correctly?

As you examine the sales pipeline, are the intended customers buying your product or service? If not, it could be that your marketing messages and channels are not reaching your target audience. It could be that improving your messaging and delivery would attract your original target customer base. That would lead to more sales growth by appealing to multiple customer segments.

The next check on your marketing strategy is around customer satisfaction. Are your customers happy with their purchases? Do they like doing business with you? Are they returning to purchase again? Are they leaving positive reviews on websites and advocating for your business? If the answer to all of these questions is not a definitive "yes," you need to dig into what is causing customers not to be loyal promoters of your business. It doesn't matter how much you spend on advertising or how good the rest of your marketing strategy is. If you don't have loyal repeat customers willing to leave positive reviews and references, your business has a problem that you must figure out before spending more time and money on your marketing strategy. It's critical to ensure that you deliver what you promised and that customers are enthusiastic about your business. This level of enthusiasm can be measured through the net promoter score.

As we've discussed throughout the book, metrics play a key role in determining whether our strategy is working. Are your metrics showing positive changes to the business? Are you getting return visitors as well as new visitors? Is revenue growing? Are you seeing a positive benefit from your marketing efforts? Does your marketing spend result in more revenue and more profit?

You can assess the efficacy of your marketing messaging and marketing channels by understanding where your consideration (leads) and conversions (sales) are coming from. What is the path that customers are taking to find you? Do you see traffic to your business coming from sources other than paid? Are they coming from referrals, from content, from your organic or owned media? How effective are you at closing a sale once you get the customer on our website or in a meeting with your salespeople? The more we can optimize the customer journey to purchase, the less money you will spend to acquire that customer, and the more profit you'll realize from sales.

If you are successful, then it's reasonable to expect your competitors to react to your success. How are your competitors responding? Are they taking actions to thwart the progress you are making or to try to answer the claims that you are making about your products or services? Competitors responding to your marketing actions is one of the best indicators that your marketing approach is working.

And finally, what are you hearing from salespeople and your distribution or channel partners? Do they see a positive change in your business? Are they seeing increased interest from prospective customers or leads truly interested in purchasing your product or service? Salespeople typically get paid commission from sales. If the marketing strategy is working, they will be getting interested from prospective customers who are serious about purchasing from them. If the marketing strategy is not working, you will likely be hearing from the sales team because their job will be much harder.

Similarly, distribution and sales partners depend on product moving and sales closing. If you are doing a good job with your strategy, that will likely support your partners' efforts. Think about your local grocery store: it's easier for the store to move products and brands that customers know. Your distribution and sales partners are good resources to check with about the effectiveness of your marketing approach. Ask them what feedback they have on your marketing strategy.

All of these are ways to know whether you are on track, but the most basic and important indicators are seeing growth in revenue, profit, and satisfied customers who return and buy more products or services from you.

Now that you've taken the journey through this book and built your marketing strategy, it's time to go for it.

You must always work to understand your business environment by understanding the competition, the suppliers, and the product features desired by your customers—and by measuring and continuously validating the segments you identified at the outset of building the marketing strategy framework. Successful marketers work to understand their market better than their competitors. You should continue to monitor your existing customers and strive to increase loyalty and advocacy. Constant testing to see that your strategy is working is essential.

Be ready to experiment with new key messages, advertising, and additional channels for the marketing content. This book is an introduction to marketing strategy, but a lot of material and services are available to help guide you as you move forward with executing your strategy. There are many resources available online and through associations such as the American Marketing Association (AMA) to further assist you in your marketing efforts, including areas such as message development, advertising development, content, and channel messaging optimization.

Where to Go Next

This book is meant to provide readers with a concise way to understand general marketing strategy, from market segmentation to measuring success. Key to this is the visual framework we introduced to help develop a marketing strategy.

The areas covered in this book and in the Strategic Marketing Framework are rich in techniques, tools, and strategies. There are a breadth and depth of approaches, methods, and tools available for the different areas covered throughout this book. We encourage you to continue exploring these areas further as you implement your marketing strategy.

It's important to understand that this book and the framework are the starting line, the entry point for developing your marketing skills. To maximize your marketing strategy, we recommend exploring other areas in depth. Those include content marketing, product development, pricing, segmentation, customer research, and the customer journey to purchase.

We hope this book has provided you with a better understanding of what's required to build out the best marketing strategy for your business. Marketing is an ongoing activity that doesn't stop with the strategy. The strategy is the scaffolding and the structure. Execution of that marketing strategy requires constant refinement and improvements. That's what makes a marketing strategy work.

Good businesses do good marketing. Great businesses constantly update their market strategy, leading to great marketing. With this book, you now have the tools to understand and build a winning marketing strategy for your business.

Appendix

Sample Strategic Marketing Framework Templates

Throughout this book, we've used the Strategic Marketing Framework along with examples of a product business (bike), a retail business (taco trailer), and a service business (tax preparation). To simplify and avoid confusing the reader, we used different examples for different sections of the book. Here are the completed Strategic Marketing Framework templates for each of these businesses.

STRATEGIC MARKETING FRAMEWORK

SEGMENT/ PRODUCT LINE Specify targets	LINE 1 Mountain Bikes		LINE 2 Road Bikes		
PEOPLE Identify and describe those you're targeting	USER Bike rider	CUSTOMER Bike rider or parent for younger bikers	USER Biker rider	CUSTOMER Bike rider or parent of younger bikers	
PRODUCT/ FEATURES Identify key products or features for users and customers	Frame type Bike size Aesthetics Component makers	Price Warranty User reviews Personalized bike fitting	Frame material and stiffness Bike size Weight Gear type	Price Warranty Breadth of options Service capability	U P S T R E A M
STRATEGIC MARKETING GOALS What are you trying to achieve?	Drive sales of higher-end mountain bikes and accessories Be seen as the <region> expert on mountain biking		Become the leader in road bike sales in the region Be the community hub for road bike activities (engagement)		
COMPETITION Who are you up against?	Online (Amazon, eBay) Bikes R Us (within 20 mi) REI Academy Outdoors		Online (Amazon, eBay) Bikes R Us (within 20 mi) Walmart, Target, Academy Outdoors		
PRICE POSITION Ideal position vs. competition or price strategy	Entry level bikes—price to big box Pro-level bikes—price skimming Accessories—cost-plus (40% GM target) Coaching and classes—value based		Entry level bikes—price to big box Pro-level bikes—price skimming Accessories—cost-plus (40% GM target) Custom fittings—value-based ($50/hr)		
KEY MESSAGES What matters to users/customers	Local—here to serve Top brands—available in store Expert mountain bike staff Competitively priced		Local—here to serve Guaranteed fit—in-store fitting Preferred Partner to local clubs Top brands—competitively priced		
PROMOTIONS/ CAMPAIGNS Get creative	Attack the mountain like a pro		The authority on <region> road biking Local newspaper Host weekly bike rides In-store fittings and training School sponsorships		

PLACEMENT Where you will run campaigns	DIGITAL *Facebook, Instagram Mountain- bike.com Google*	TRADITIONAL *Local newspaper MTB club visits MTB pop-ups at local trails*	DIGITAL *Facebook, Instagram, YouTube Cycling .com Google*	TRADITIONAL *Local newspaper Host weekly bike rides In-store fittings School sponsorships*	D O W N S T R E A M
SUCCESS MEASURES How you will measure progress	*Revenue growth rate Customer return rate Net promoter score*		*Revenue growth rate Customer return rate Net promoter score*		
NOTES	*Overall goal is to attract and retain serious mountain bikers—higher end product and margins*		*Drive to attract bikers in the beginning of their biking—long term customer engagement*		

Figure A.1 Bike business template

STRATEGIC MARKETING FRAMEWORK

SEGMENT/ PRODUCT LINE Specify targets	LINE 1 Taco Trailer Walkup Business		LINE 2 Delivery services (e.g., Doordash, Uber Eats)		
PEOPLE Identify and describe those you're targeting	USER *Individuals Families Couples*	CUSTOMER *Person who pays for the tacos*	USER *Meeting attendees, event goers, etc*	CUSTOMER *Person who selects and orders for the delivery*	
PRODUCT/ FEATURES Identify key products or features for users and customers	*Choice of tacos Dietary options Quality of food Taste of food*	*Same as user Price Speed of availability*	*Choice of tacos Dietary options Packaging Taste and quality*	*Cost Timing Accuracy of order Ease of serving Happiness of attendees*	U P S T R E A M
STRATEGIC MARKETING GOALS What are you trying to achieve?	*Become a destination trailer for foodies Build a loyal following of happy customers*		*Drive higher profitability by larger order services (more revenue, less overhead costs) Expand brand awareness by exposing prospective customers through catering*		
COMPETITION Who are you up against?	*Mexican restaurants Fast food restaurants Other food trailers*		*Caterers Restaurants using delivery services Delivery service platforms*		
PRICE POSITION Ideal position vs. competition or price strategy	*Specialty tacos—premium pricing (price skimming) Standard tacos—competitively priced to other tacos in the area*		*Price to catering competition— competitive pricing (be equal to or within 5% of other caterers doing taco catering)*		
KEY MESSAGES What matters to users/customers	*Tasty, quality tacos Cooked to order Local and foodie favorite Unique offerings*		*Caterers Restaurants using delivery services Delivery service platforms*		
PROMOTIONS/ CAMPAIGNS Get creative	*Best tacos you can get in (area)*		*Simplify and Tacofy your event to delight you guests*		

PLACEMENT Where you will run campaigns	DIGITAL *Google* *Facebook,* *Instagram,* *Yelp* *Food blogs*	TRADITIONAL *Local newspaper* *Local sponsorships*	DIGITAL *Google* *Website* *Facebook,* *Instagram,* *Yelp* *Food Blogs* *Uber Eats/* *Doordash*	TRADITIONAL *Direct Mail* *Chamber of* *Commerce* *Communications*	D O W N S
SUCCESS MEASURES How you will measure progress	*Cost per impression and* *conversions* *Reviews and ratings* *Repeat purchase growth* *Revenue growth rate*		*Cost per click and conversions* *Customer return rate* *Average revenue per transaction* *Reviews and ratings*		T R E A M
NOTES	*Drive the amount of transac-* *tions and dollars per transac-* *tion, minimize the amount of* *quiet time at the trailer*		*Maximize the side of orders so* *that more tacos are sold per order* *to increase revenue with limited* *overhead costs*		

Figure A.2 Taco trailer template

STRATEGIC MARKETING FRAMEWORK

SEGMENT/ PRODUCT LINE Specify targets	LINE 1 Business Customers (bookkeeping and tax)		LINE 2 Individual Tax Preparation		
PEOPLE Identify and describe those you're targeting	USER Executives Board Members Tax Authorities Lenders (banks)	CUSTOMER Bus < 25 employees Finance or accounting reporting	USER Individuals Spouse (filing jointly or family)	CUSTOMER Person responsible for tax filing	
PRODUCT/ FEATURES Identify key products or features for users and customers	Reliable financial reports Tax filings on time Timely availability	Cost Guidance on tax planning Reliability No tax or report issues	Complete-ness of return Maximizing refunds/lim-iting taxes due	Cost Timing/Accuracy Maximizing refunds/limiting taxes due	U P S T R E A M
STRATEGIC MARKETING GOALS What are you trying to achieve?	Building deep, long-term engagements with businesses Earn trust to do more than just tax or reporting services		Win against DIY and retail tax prep services Build a year over year return tax relationship		
COMPETITION Who are you up against?	National accounting firms Other local firms Online accounting systems (DIY)		Retail tax preparers Other local tax preparers Online tax prep platforms Tax preparation software		
PRICE POSITION Ideal position vs. competition or price strategy	Engagement contracts competitive pricing (less than national firms, equal to local firms) Social projects—cost plus pricing (billable time plus expenses)		Annual tax filing—competitive pricing (equal to retail firms) Advising—value based (hourly fee) Storage of tax return info cost plus for storage fee plus a markup		
KEY MESSAGES What matters to users/customers	Deep financial and accounting expertise Cost-effective Responsive and reliable Broad technical capabilities		Experienced tax preparers History of happy customers Quality work Fast service		
PROMOTIONS/ CAMPAIGNS Get creative	Start the fiscal year right with the accounting services partner (Q4 push)		Minimize your tax burden, minimize your stress (November and March campaigns)		

PLACEMENT Where you will run campaigns	DIGITAL Google/ adwords Business website LinkedIn	TRADITIONAL Local newspaper Chamber of commerce ads Local business press Local sponsorships Local radio (sports?)	DIGITAL Facebook, Yelp Google Business Website	TRADITIONAL Local Newspaper Neighborhood newsletters Local radio Referrals Local school sponsorships	D O W N S
SUCCESS MEASURES How you will measure progress	Cost per click and conversions Customer lifetime value Retention rate (churn rate) Average revenue per customer		Cost per impression and conversions Customer return rate Net promoter score		T R E A
NOTES	Goal is to build ongoing billable relationships with customers. Be considered a part of the internal team.		Be trusted source for tax preparation. Drive customer loyalty and encourage advocacy to attract new customers.		M

Figure A.3 Tax preparation template

Bibliography

American Marketing Association. 2022. *Definitions of Marketing*. www.ama.org/the-definition-of-marketing-what-is-marketing (accessed March 9, 2023).

Bain & Company. 2023. "Measuring Your Net Promoter Score." *Net Promoter System*. www.netpromotersystem.com/about/measuring-your-net-promoter-score/ (accessed March 13, 2023).

Baskin Robbins CA. March 2016. *Baskin-Robbins Launches Warm Cookie Ice Cream Sandwiches and Sundaes*. www.baskinrobbins.ca/press-releases/baskin-robbins-launches-warm-cookie-ice-cream-sandwiches-and-sundaes (accessed March 9, 2023).

Charan, R. 2004. *Profitable Growth Is Everyone's Business: 10 Tools You Can Use Monday Morning*. 1st ed. New York, NY: Currency.

Chen, B.X. 2020. "Up To 91% More Expensive: How Delivery Apps Eat Up Your Budget." *The New York Times*, sec. Technology. www.nytimes.com/2020/02/26/technology/personaltech/ubereats-doordash-postmates-grubhub-review.html (accessed March 9, 2023).

Dictionary.com, s.v. 2023. "Sale." www.dictionary.com/browse/sale (accessed March 9, 2023).

Gallo, A. 2014. "The Value of Keeping the Right Customers." *Harvard Business Review*. https://hbr.org/2014/10/the-value-of-keeping-the-right-customers (accessed March 13, 2023).

Gundlach, G.T. 2007. "The American Marketing Association's 2004 Definition of Marketing: Perspectives on Its Implications for Scholarship and the Role and Responsibility of Marketing in Society." *Journal of Public Policy & Marketing* 26, no. 2, pp. 243–250.

Irvine, M. 2022. "Google Ads Benchmarks for YOUR Industry." *Wordstream.com*. www.wordstream.com/blog/ws/2016/02/29/google-adwords-industry-benchmarks (accessed March 9, 2023).

Kotler Marketing Group Inc. 2019. *Dr. Philip Kotler Answers Your Questions on Marketing*. https://kotlermarketing.com/phil_questions.shtml#answer3 (accessed March 9, 2023).

Kotler, P. and K.L. Keller. 2012. *Marketing Management*. 14th ed. Upper Saddle River, New Jersey, NJ: Pearson Education, Inc. publishing as Prentice Hall.

McCarthy, E.J. 1960. *Basic Marketing: A Managerial Approach*. Homewood, Illinois, IL: R.D. Irwin.

Porter, M.E. January 2008. "The Five Competitive Forces That Shape Strategy." *Harvard Business Review*.

Savar, A. 2013. *Content to Commerce: Engaging Consumers Across Paid, Owned and Earned Channels.* Hoboken, New Jersey, NJ: Wiley.

Solomon, D. and P. Forbes. August 2020. "No Store Did More: How H-E-B Became a Model of Emergency Preparedness." *Texas Monthly.*

Statista.com. 2022. "McDonald's Corporation's Advertising Costs From 2014 to 2021 (in Million U.S. Dollars)." www.statista.com/statistics/286541/mcdonald-s-advertising-spending-worldwide/ (accessed March 9, 2023).

Statista.com. 2021. "Number of Baskin-Robbins Stores Worldwide From 2007 to 2019, by Region." www.statista.com/statistics/291474/distribution-points-baskin-robbins/ (accessed March 9, 2023).

Strong, E.K., Jr. 1925. *The Psychology of Selling and Advertising.* New York, NY: McGraw-Hill Book Company, Inc.

Whalen, D.J. and K.K. Coker. May 2016. "Outside the Box Teaching Moments: Classroom-Tested Innovations." *Marketing Education Review* 26, no. 2, pp. 119–123.

About the Authors

Dr. David Altounian is the Vice Provost of Graduate and Professional Studies and an Associate Professor of Entrepreneurship at Salve Regina University in Newport, Rhode Island. He has over 30 years of leading marketing and operations organizations in the technology sector with leading companies including Motion Computing, Dell, Motorola, Compaq Computer Corporation, and Ashton-Tate. He is a partner and mentor at Capital Factory, a leading entrepreneurial center in Austin, Texas. Dr. Altounian earned his Ph.D. at Oklahoma State University and his MBA at the Kellogg School of Management at Northwestern University.

Mike Cronin is a Peabody, duPont, and Murrow award-winning journalist with experience spanning more than two decades. Cronin's beats have included startups, finance, growth, and the economy. He also has advised companies on developing content, media, market positioning, messaging, and growth public-relations strategies. Cronin earned a master's degree in international affairs from Columbia University in New York City and a bachelor's degree in politics from Trinity College in Dublin, Ireland.

Index

OTHER TITLES IN THE MARKETING COLLECTION

Naresh Malhotra, Georgia Tech, Editor

- *Marketing of Consumer Financial Products* by Ritu Srivastava
- *The Big Miss* by Zhecho Dobrev
- *Digital Brand Romance* by Anna Harrison
- *Brand Vision* by James Everhart
- *Brand Naming* by Rob Meyerson
- *Fast Fulfillment* by Sanchoy Das
- *Multiply Your Business Value Through Brand & AI* by Rajan Narayan
- *Branding & AI* by Chahat Aggarwal
- *The Business Design Cube* by Rajagopal
- *Customer Relationship Management* by Michael Pearce
- *The Coming Age of Robots* by George Pettinico and George R. Milne
- *Market Entropy* by Rajagopal
- *Decoding Customer Value at the Bottom of the Pyramid* by Ritu Srivastava
- *Qualitative Marketing Research* by Rajagopal
- *Social Media Marketing* by Alan Charlesworth
- *Employee Ambassadorship* by Michael W Lowenstein

Concise and Applied Business Books

The Collection listed above is one of 30 business subject collections that Business Expert Press has grown to make BEP a premiere publisher of print and digital books. Our concise and applied books are for...

- Professionals and Practitioners
- Faculty who adopt our books for courses
- Librarians who know that BEP's Digital Libraries are a unique way to offer students ebooks to download, not restricted with any digital rights management
- Executive Training Course Leaders
- Business Seminar Organizers

Business Expert Press books are for anyone who needs to dig deeper on business ideas, goals, and solutions to everyday problems. Whether one print book, one ebook, or buying a digital library of 110 ebooks, we remain the affordable and smart way to be business smart. For more information, please visit www.businessexpertpress.com, or contact sales@businessexpertpress.com.